# The FOCALGUIDE to Photographing People

# THE ⓕ FOCALGUIDES TO

| | |
|---|---|
| THE 35mm SINGLE LENS REFLEX | Leonard Gaunt |
| HOME PROCESSING | Ralph Jacobson |
| ENLARGING | Günter Spitzing |
| PORTRAITS | Günter Spitzing |
| FLASH | Günter Spitzing |
| EFFECTS AND TRICKS | Günter Spitzing |
| MOVIEMAKING | Paul Petzold |
| 35mm | Leonard Gaunt |
| COLOUR | David Lynch |
| FILTERS | Clyde Reynolds |
| COLOUR PRINTING | Jack Coote |
| LOW LIGHT PHOTOGRAPHY | Paul Petzold |
| CAMERAS | Clyde Reynolds |
| LIGHTING | Paul Petzold |
| LENSES | Leonard Gaunt |
| MOUNTAINS | Douglas Milner |
| SHOOTING ANIMATION | Zoran Perisic |
| PHOTOGRAPHING PEOPLE | Alison Trapmore |

# The FOCALGUIDE to Photographing People

Alison Trapmore

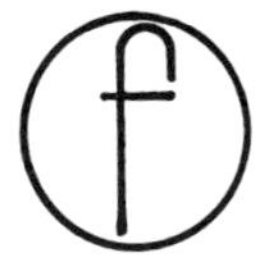

Focal Press
London & New York

ISBN 0 240 50972 2

**British Library Cataloguing in Publication Data**

Trapmore, Alison
The focalguide to photographing people.
1. Photography – Portraits – Amateurs' manuals
I. Title
778.9'2 TR575

ISBN 0–240–50972–2

Reproduced and printed by photolithography and bound in Great Britain at The Pitman Press, Bath

# Contents

# Introduction

This book is about people first and cameras second because you need imagination and an eye for detail to take successful pictures of people rather than lots of expensive photographic gear. The guide shows you how to develop these qualities so that you can see good pictures in every day happenings like the kids at play in the back garden or the shoppers in the market place. It teaches you to anticipate people's actions as well as their moods and fleeting expressions in order to capture really effective pictures.

The book explains how to select the most appropriate camera angles and shooting distances for picturing people of different ages in both candid as well as formal situations; how to look at a scene and then distinguish between relevant and irrelevant details; how to arrange pictures simply and creatively; how to see lighting in terms of its nature and direction so that you can manipulate it to advantage; and, most important of all, how to take natural spontaneous pictures of people that you'll be proud of.

Some readers will be particularly interested in getting a few ideas on taking pictures that will create satisfying personal memories of the children and family happenings. Others will want to venture into the realms of more creative photography and discover the whys and wherefores of picture composition and candid camera techniques. Perhaps some readers will want to explore the possibilities of taking pictures that have universal appeal, the sort of shots that will be hung in camera club exhibitions and win photo competitions.

Whatever your reason for wanting to find out more about photographing people it is hoped that the ideas in this book will help you to realise your ambitions. Once you get into the swing of things, having mastered the technicalities of your camera, you'll find it fascinating to study people's actions and expressions in numerous different situations. You will certainly have lots of fun when you go out and about with your camera and begin to capture relaxed pictures of people that are good to look at and satisfying to have taken.

# Taking Photographs

To take good pictures of people, or any other subject for that matter, you have to know enough about your camera and photography to be able to forget the technicalities and get on with making pictures. Most of the basic skills required for making good pictures depend on common sense things which are almost second nature to the advanced photographer who has mastered the use of his camera. To the less experienced camera owner however, they form the base of the pyramid on which he can develop his creative skills.

## Know your camera

The first step towards creating successful pictures of people is to get to know every detail of your camera so that you can use it almost without thinking. When this happens you will be able to concentrate on the people you are photographing rather than on the camera. You will find it much easier to capture natural actions when you don't have to hestitate over technicalities.

If you have never really bothered to learn the ins and outs of your camera, or if you have just acquired a new model, examine it carefully with the instruction book close at hand. Go through all the operating instructions slowly and deliberately, checking each written instruction with the appropriate part of the camera. Practise using the camera when there's no film inside so you get used to the weight and the feel of it. If you have a 35mm camera look through the viewfinder with the body held first horizontally and then vertically so that you get accustomed to the different grips and arm positions that the two views require. For most of your pictures of people you'll want to use the vertical format rather than the horizontal view. Human features generally fit more neatly into a vertical frame.

When you have become used to handling the camera at eye level go through the operating sequence of setting the exposure, viewing the subject, focusing the lens and releasing the shutter. The more times you can practise this with actual people in front of the lens the better. After a while you should find that the actions of the operating sequence will begin to feel easy and to flow naturally.

While you are practising using your camera stand with your feet apart so that you can hold the camera firmly. If you get into the habit of standing correctly whenever you use the camera you should be all set to take a picture whenever an opportunity presents itself. The moment this happens draw in your breath and press the shutter release gently. The action should be smooth and easy to ensure that the camera is held quite still the moment the picture is made. If you stab at the shutter release or hold the camera awkwardly you are liable to get unsharp pictures. This unsharpness affects the entire image area and should not be confused with subject movement which causes the subject to be unsharp and not the surrounding picture area. If you are doubtful about one or two points when you have been through the camera operating instructions a few times, the best thing to do is to take the camera and the instruction booklet along to your local photographic dealer. He will probably be pleased to sort things out for you particularly if you call at a slack time of day rather than at lunchtime or on a Saturday when he's rushed off his feet.

Once you fully understand the technicalities of your camera the easiest way of finding out exactly what it will do and what it won't do is to take pictures with it.

## The viewfinder

The camera viewfinder is an extremely important feature of picture making. It is the place where pictures are created before they become real photographs, where the effects of all the donkey work of picture arranging is considered and amended. It is where, too, when you are photographing people, you watch their activities to see just the right moment to press the shutter release.

While you are composing a shot in the viewfinder, keep important details away from the edge of the frame. Slight masking of the image area always occurs during slide mounting or printing so that you may lose the outermost edges of the picture. Group pictures, particularly wedding groups where it's a squeeze to picture the whole assembly outside the church, frequently appear with an unfortunate trim through the figures at each end of the line up. This is emphasised in prints made from 35mm negatives as they never contain the full width of the negative image. The only way to avoid the problem is to increase the camera-to-subject distance so that there is space around the essential part of the picture.

Because the viewfinder is such an important part of creating good pictures you need to be certain that you are using it correctly. This is not the case if your pictures have consistently shown one of the following faults:

1. The people seem further away than you remember them being
2. An important part of the subject is cut off both at the top and the side in a close-up portrait
3. Part of the top of the head is missing in a close-up portrait.

A run down on the causes of these faults and other viewfinding problems is given in the Technical Tips on page 174.

## Choose the right film

There is a wide range of different types and makes of film to choose from. The one you select should be the most suitable for photographing people in a particular situation with your particular camera.

Most inexpensive cameras will only take medium-speed films as they are geared for ease of use rather than flexibility. The same three different types of film are available for these cameras as for their more versatile relations – these give colour prints, colour slides or black-and-white prints. However, if you want to make sure of getting a high proportion of reasonably exposed pictures it's preferable to use negative films for photographing people with a simple camera. That's because negative films, either black-and-white or colour, are fairly tolerant to inaccurate exposure. Correction can usually be made

at the printing stage for any exposure errors that you do happen to make. Colour slide films on the other hand need to be accurately exposed to give good results for there is no easy way of correcting for over or under-exposure once a picture has been taken.
Just to complete the picture; you can get black-and-white transparency films, but they are not widly used these days.

## Films for adjustable cameras

Adjustable cameras (i.e. those with exposure controls on them) can be used with slow, medium or fast films; but for photographing people you really need a medium speed or a fast film. Medium-speed films are generally used for summer photography outdoors. Fast films are the ideal choice for recording action shots and candid pictures of people particularly in the winter when lighting levels tend to be quite low. Fast films with high film speed numbers allow you maximum flexibility in your choice of lens aperture and shutter speed settings under a wide range of lighting conditions.
Slow films, with film speed numbers lower than 40 ASA, are capable of recording extremely fine detail. They are generally used to record top quality images that are intended to be viewed with considerable enlargement such as large studio portraits and big screen 35mm transparencies. Slow films are not sufficiently sensitive to light to allow you to shoot quickly with fast shutter speeds and capture lively and interesting pictures of people.
More detailed information on the characteristics of colour and black-and-white films is given in the chapter 'Photographic Technicalities', on pages 193–198.

## The low down on film speeds

Most adjustable cameras have an exposure meter built in; and simple hand-held or close-up meters are readily available for use with those that don't. Exposure meters measure levels of light and enable you to convert the measurements into camera exposure settings. These settings are sometimes more accurate than the figures

given in the film instruction sheet, especially when the subject is close to the camera or the lighting is unusual.
All exposure meters need to be programmed with a single piece of descriptive information before they can give correct exposure settings. This information is supplied on the film carton in the form of a film speed or meter setting number with the prefix ASA/BS or DIN. The ASA/BS number is for use with meters calibrated for British or American Standard indices. The DIN scale is based on the German standard. There is an equivalent DIN value for each ASA/BS speed. However, the ASA/BS numbers are easier to use as they increase arithmetically whereas the DIN scale is based on logarithmic units. The higher the film speed number, the faster the film (i.e. the greater as its sensitivity to light).

TYPICAL FILM SPEEDS

| Speed category | Colour films | Black-and-white films |
|---|---|---|
| Slow | Up to 40ASA | Up to 40ASA |
| Medium | 50–100ASA | 50–200ASA |
| Fast | 125–250ASA | 250–800ASA |
| Ultra fast | 320–500ASA | 1000ASA and over |

A film that is double the ASA speed of another is twice as sensitive to light. For example, a film with an ASA speed of 100 can be correctly exposed by half as much light as one rated at 50 ASA. In terms of aperture settings that's equivalent to one stop, so instead of shooting at 1/125 second at *f*5.6 on a 50 ASA film you could shoot at 1/125 second at *f*8 (or 1/250 second at *f*5.6) using a 100 ASA film in the same lighting conditions. The faster shutter speed is nearly always an advantage when you are photographing people.

## Colour or black-and-white?

As to choosing between colour or black-and-white films there is no doubt that colour is the first choice even though it's more expensive than black-and-white. It's worth every extra penny to have natural and colourful life-like pictures which are encouraging to look at and a pleasure to show to other people. Black-and-white films are fine for the youngsters to experiment with and necessary for the serious amateur to enable him to discover the monochromatic art. If you are finding it difficult to decide whether to use colour slide or colour print films with your adjustable camera, the pros and cons of both are discussed on page 192. Once you get used to making accurate exposures in different lighting conditions with one particular kind of film it is best to stick with it for a while. When there is a familiar film in your camera you have a chance to concentrate on the people you are photographing rather than on exposure technicalities. The time to experiment with new and different films is when you are creating successful pictures on the film to which you have become accustomed.

## Find the right sort of light

Photography is all about light and to make successful, well exposed pictures of people you obviously need a fair amount of it. Besides affecting camera exposure, light also influences the appearance of people in your pictures. You will find that in some lighting conditions photography is easy and your pictures flatter the people you have photographed. In other lighting conditions it seems more of an effort to use the camera and it takes really powerful, action packed situations to make successful photographs.

## The ideal lighting for photographing people

Generally, the most natural pictures of people are taken outdoors on cloudy or hazy days when the lighting is partially or totally diffused. In conditions like these there is usually a bit of direction to the light so any shadows are soft and gentle in outline. Photography is easy because neither you nor the people you are photographing are bothering about the sun so the whole situation is relaxed and natural. You can point your camera in any direction you fancy without having to consider the adverse effects of high contrast brought about by the highlights and shadows of bright sun shining on the scene.

## Sunlight

On bright sunny days, people frequently go about with squints and deep furrows set on their faces to protect their eyes against the sun. In direct sunlight it's more difficult to capture spontaneously natural pictures particularly of children who, at an early age, seem to have perfected the technique of facial contortion in order to carry on regardless however bright the light. Because of this it is none too easy to take good pictures of energetic youngsters on bright sunny days. If you want to make certain of really successful results you need to manoeuvre things so that you manage to photograph the children when they are facing away from the sun or so that the action happens in the shade. The lighting underneath a tree or on the shadow side of a building is far better for photographing people than direct sunshine.

Older people are much easier than children to photograph on sunny days. They tend to do the sensible thing and either congregate for conversations in spots that are shaded from the sun or face the glare under the protection of a wide-brimmed hat or sunglasses.

You can study the effects of sunlight quite easily without a camera. All you need to do is to go outside on a sunny day, see the direction of the sun and note how its light affects people and their surroundings.

## Front lighting

You will notice that when the sun is shining directly onto people's faces it causes discomfort and grimaces. the lighting does nothing to enhance facial features; it's flat as well as being harsh so your subject tends to look rather pudding-like, with 'stuck-on' features. The deep black shadows in the eye-sockets and under the nose and chin are most unflattering. The harsh effects of sunlight are at a maximum in the middle of the day when the sun is high in the sky and in the mid-summer months. At these times front lighting is unsuitable for making successful close-ups of people.

## Side lighting

When the sun is shining onto the side of someone nearby, you will see the characteristic nose shadow which typifies side lighting. The variations in tones across the face emphasise contours and skin textures. This facial shaping (photographers call it 'modelling') is totally lacking with front lighting. Although side lighting is quite satisfactory for close up pictures of people, the shadows tend to give unnecessarily complicated results with middle distance and long shots. This applies particularly to photographs of groups of people. Also, because of the violent contrast between the highlights of the sunlit areas and the relatively deep shadows that are a characteristic of side lighting, you must choose your viewpoint and lighting angles with great care.

## Back lighting

As you screw up your eyes to see the effects of back lighting you may be able to appreciate the photographic problems it causes. In spite of the brightness of the light shining towards you, the effects of the back lighting on nearby people are soft and totally diffused. The lighting gives skin tones an almost translucent quality which can be extremely flattering. To ensure successful photographs with back lighting you need to use a lens hood to shade the camera lens from the direct rays of the sun. In addition, you need to give your picture extra exposure – the sun is shining on you and your camera and not on your subject, who is effectively in the shade.

On sunny days, particularly during the summer months, experienced photographers try not to take pictures around noon when the sun is high in the sky and creating heavy shadows and harsh contrasts. It is almost impossible to take good pictures of people under these conditions. Close up photographs are particularly unflattering with heavy uncomplimentary shadows around the eyes and nose. It's far

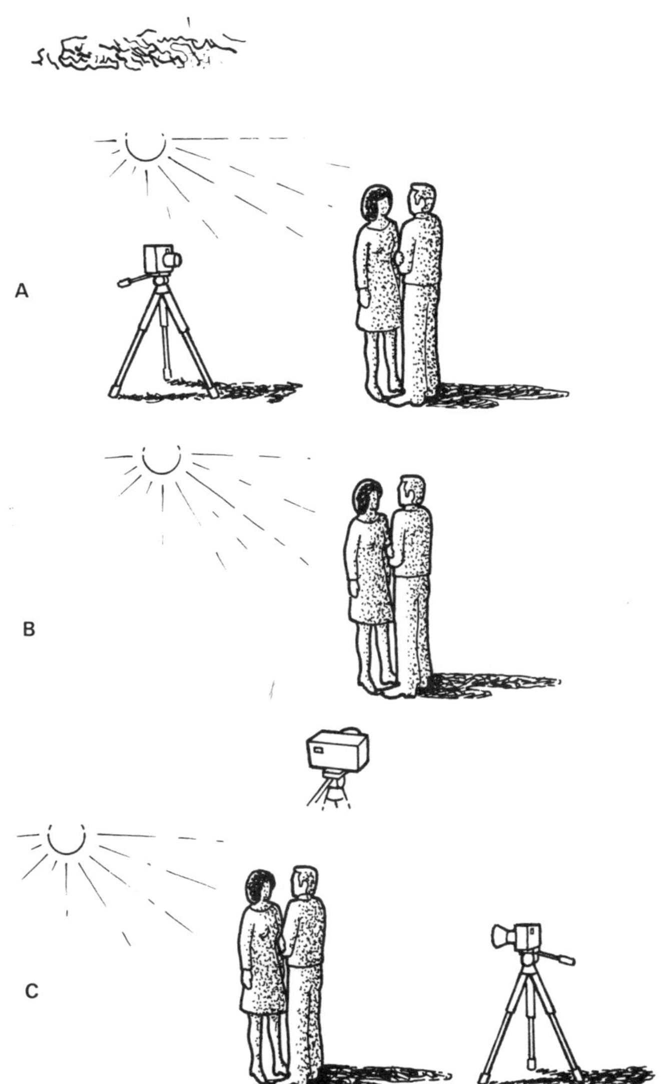


Sunlight from different angles. A. Front lighting (light behind camera shining onto subject). B. Side lighting (light shining onto side of camera and subject). C. Back lighting (light shining towards camera).

better to concentrate on picture taking in the morning or afternoon when the sun is lower in the sky and it's effects are less severe. Over the page is a summary of the advantages and disadvantages of direct sunlight.

EXPOSURE FOR BACK-LIT SUBJECTS

| Colour negative film (Film speed 80ASA) | Normal exposure for bright or hazy sun | Exposure for back-lit subjects near to the camera |
|---|---|---|
| Adjustable camera setting* | 1/25 sec, *f*11 | 1/125 sec, *f*5.6<br>OR<br>1/60 sec, *f*8 |
| Simple camera setting | Bright sun symbol | Cloudy bright symbol |

*If your camera is fitted with through-the-lens metering, or if you use any other exposure system that measures average scene brightness, you need to go in close to the subject to get an accurate indication of the required exposure for a back-lit subject.

SUMMARY OF THE ADVANTAGES AND DISADVANTAGES OF DIRECT SUNLIGHT

| | Front lighting | Side lighting | Back lighting |
|---|---|---|---|
| Photographic Advantages | Gives perfect colour rendition | Good for record shots of people and events | Good for close-ups and silhouettes |
| Photographic Disadvantages | Unsuitable for close-ups of people | Shadows can be harsh | Exposure needs care |

**Lighting indoors**

Although it's not generally possible to be quite so casual about photographing people indoors as in the bright light outdoors, that

| | Flash-on-camera | Flash-off-camera (bounced or umbrella) | Available light |
|---|---|---|---|
| Suitable films | Any | Any, fairly powerful unit | High-speed films |
| Light | Direct | Soft and diffused | Generally directional |
| Flash | Any | Generally | – |
| Camera | Any | Adjustable cameras | Adjustable cameras, preferably with a wide-aperture lens |
| Additional equipment | None or simple flashgun | Extension lead, photographic umbrella | A light meter if one is not an integral part of your camera |
| Applications | Limited to record shots | Numerous, but particularly suitable for semi-posed pictures | Excellent for informal candid photography. |

doesn't mean to say it's impossible to capture natural pictures of happenings in and around the home. It simply means that you have to tailor your approach to each particular situation to suit your camera and lighting gear. To help you do this the following table summarises the different factors involved:

If you are not used to taking pictures indoors or are unfamiliar with any of the terms or techniques mentioned in the table, more information is given in the flash facts on page 182 and in the section on available light on page 25.

It's far more difficult to take natural pictures of people indoors because there is usually insufficient light for you to be able to use your camera without having to boost the level of illumination with flash. This applies particularly if you only have a simple camera which has few, if any, adjustments on it. An adjustable camera, especially one fitted with a wide aperture lens, offers much greater scope for experimenting with indoor photography. You can use it for taking pictures by available light as well as for capturing scenes lit by the diffused lighting of bounced or umbrella flash.

### Flash-on-camera

The easiest way of shooting pictures with flash, and the way to extend the picture taking possibilities of a simple camera, is to have the light-source attached to the camera itself. With the majority of inexpensive modern cameras, a flash socket is an integral part of the camera body. This makes flash photography simple and convenient. All you need to do is to pop a flashcube or magicube into the socket and you are ready for action. The four tiny flashbulbs contained within the cube enable you to take four pictures in rapid succession – it's as easy as that.

Flash-on-camera is the sort of lighting that most people use for taking fun pictures of family happenings and to commemorate special occasions like Christmas and birthdays as well as for recording shots of the children around the home for the photo album. The effect of the light produced by the flash is very similar to that of direct sunshine, it's bright and harsh and casts fairly heavy shadows. Unfortunately, the shadows are often more noticeable on indoor flash shots than they are on pictures taken outdoors in direct sunlight. That's because there is often a wall fairly close to people featured in indoor pictures; all ready to receive a few shapely shadows cast by the figures in front. Outdoors, shadows cast by the sunlight are usually free to fall on the ground and in such a position are far less obtrusive. The table on page 183 tells you how to minimise the effects of shadows and gives easy remedies to other flash-on-camera problems.

### Flash-off-camera

Adjustable cameras usually have provision for more versatile flash facilities than those afforded by the flash-on-camera attachments of

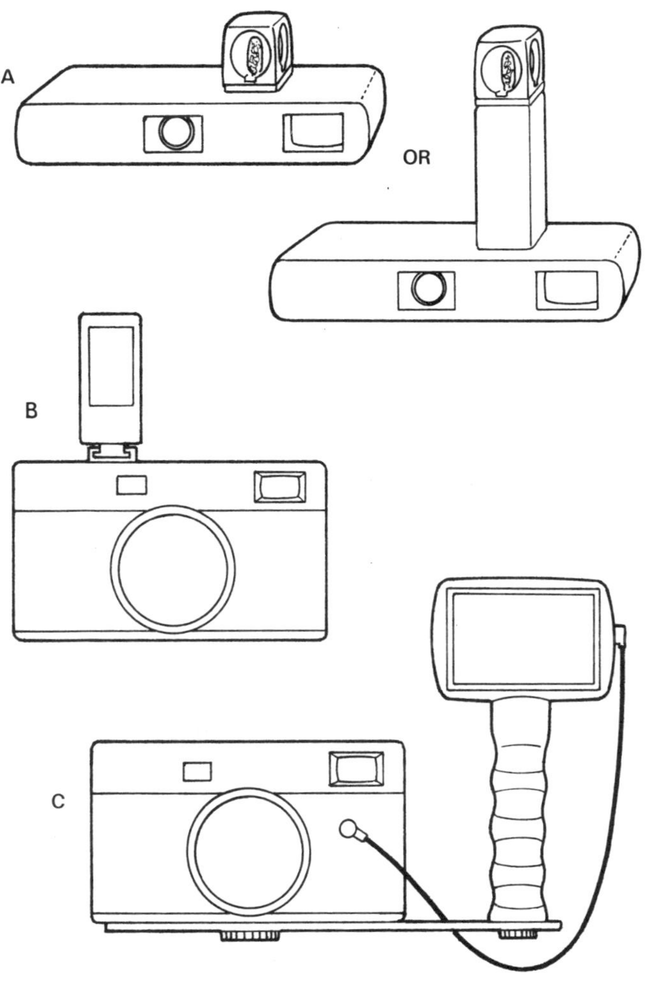


Pathways to flash. A & B Built-in systems for easy shooting. C. Separate flash off-camera for natural lighting and creative photography.

inexpensive models. That's because the rather harsh light of direct flash is not favoured by the specialist who will want to control the light to create special effects or to simulate the diffused illumination of overcast daylight which is so good for photographing people. To do any of these things, the flash needs to be positioned some way away from the camera.

The easiest way of working with the flash off the camera is simply to hold it at arms length pointing downwards onto the people you are photographing. Used in this way the flash will produce lighting that is similar to side lighting (over the shoulder) on a bright sunny day. The main time that this direct flash-off-camera technique really comes into its own is for taking pictures of groups of people at parties and other social gatherings where you want to distribute the light more evenly than would be possible when using flash-on-camera. The disadvantages of this directional lighting are that you need a helper or a tripod to hold the flashgun in a suitable place; and even though the effects are often better than with flash-on-camera, it still gives rather harsh, shadowy results.

Experienced photographers achieve more natural-looking pictures of people indoors by diffusing the flash light to give soft, even illumination that is more flattering to the subject than direct flash. There are two methods of using a single light source to provide diffused lighting, bounced flash and Paraflash. With bounced lighting the diffusing surface is a wall or ceiling and with Paraflash it is a white umbrella. (The name Paraflash is given to the complete unit which consists of a folding umbrella connected to an attachment containing a shoe holder for the flashgun and a screw thread for fiitting the unit onto a tripod head.) Both methods give excellent lighting for photographing babies and young children as well as groups of people. They are illustrated in the diagram on page 187 and more detailed information about exposures and other technical tips is given on page 183.

**Available light**

"Available light" is the photographic term used to describe picture taking in existing illumination. It is usual to associate low levels of illumination with available light rather than normal daylight. Window lighting, candle light, fire light and conventional domestic lighting all come within the specialised sphere of available light.

There are several advantages of using available light rather than flashbulbs to light the scene:

. It's economical because you don't need elaborate or expensive flash equipment

. It's fun and provides lots of scope for the adventurous, creative photographer

. You can see the effects of the light in the camera viewfinder before you take the picture which is something you cannot do with flash

.Because it's a natural form of lighting, its effects are realistic and often exciting.

However, because there is not much light, you need a "fast" lens (that's one with a maximum aperture in the region of *f*2.8 or *f*1.4) with a range of shutter speeds down to about $\frac{1}{4}$ second. Then, with high speed films, your equipment can be used in the very dimmest of conditions. If you are unfamiliar with the techniques of available light photography a summary of the basic requirements is given on page 189.

**Exposure**

Camera exposure is a bit like sunbathing – if you strike the correct balance between the length of time you sit in the sun and the strength of the sunlight, you should acquire an even tan. Good pictures require a similar well balanced exposure. The time, usually measured in fractions of a second, is controlled by the camera shutter; and the strength or intensity of the light by the lens aperture. When the balance between the two is correct the film is well exposed.

Unlike the sunbather, the photographer doesn't necessarily need bright sun to practise his art. He can get well exposed pictures under a great variety of lighting conditions simply by adjusting the shutter speed and lens aperture controls of his camera and making full use of the different types of film that are available.

To be able to to this he needs a fully adjustable camera as

opposed to a simple, inexpensive model that was designed for easy shooting rather than for flexibility. Many basic snapshot cameras have few, if any, adjustments on them and can only be used with a limited range of films.

The simplest of such cameras have a fixed-aperture lens and a single-speed shutter. They are geared to give correct exposure only in bright sunshine or by the equally powerful light of a flashbulb illuminating subjects up to about 3m (10 feet away). These lighting conditions are fine for recording family snapshots but are too limiting for adventurous photography of people.

However, if you have a camera without any adjustments on it you will have an excellent chance of making good pictures provided you confine your efforts to photographing people in well-lit situations. It is best to steer clear of action-packed close-ups of the children performing on the swings and roundabouts or similar subjects that require faster than average shutter speeds to capture a sharp image. And, when there is no sun to create a well-exposed image, you will need to use flash (outdoors on dull, cloudy days as well as indoors).

There are a number of slightly more versatile cameras which, although basically simple, have a few adjustments on them in the form of weather symbols. These are very easy to set to give the correct exposure and the cameras are effortless to use. They are the sort of cameras that photographically-orientated families use as a convenient alternative to their more elaborate reflex model which is rather too precious to leave lying around in anticipation of the odd unexpected happening. Versatile but inexpensive cameras are particularly useful for recording scenes of the children around the home for the family album.

## Apertures and shutter speeds

The correct exposure for any picture taken on an adjustable camera is the most appropriate combination of shutter speed and lens aperture to suit the subject, the lighting conditions and the film in use. A standard combination of shutter speed and lens aperture for a series of different lighting conditions from bright sun to cloudy dull is given in every film instruction sheet. A typical set of figures for a medium-speed, colour slide film reads:

Meter Settings: ASSA/BS 64, 19 DIN

| Bright or hazy sun on light sand or snow | Bright or hazy sun (distinct shadows) | Weak hazy sun (soft shadows) | Cloudy bright (no shadows) | Open shade or cloudy dull |
|---|---|---|---|---|
| *f*16 1/125 sec | *f*11 1/125 sec | *f*8 1/125 sec | *f*5.6 1/125 sec | *f*4 1/125 sec |

A shutter speed of 1/25 second is fine for general photography involving fairly static subjects which can be tackled at a fairly leisurely pace but it's a bit slow for photographing people on the move. If you want to capture candid shots of people doing interesting things and to take close-ups of people with relaxed and natural expressions, you will need to work quickly and to take pictures fairly rapidly. If the lighting conditions allow, it's better to shoot at 1/250th or even 1/500th second. At these faster shutter speeds your pictures will not show the effects of slight camera shake or subject movement both of which can happen when you are photographing people in natural situations.

A fast shutter speed is also an advantage if you are using a camera fitted with a heavy telephoto lens or an equally weighty zoom lens. The heavier your equipment, the more difficult it is to hold steady during an exposure. What's more, long focus lenses don't just magnify the subject, they magnify the effects of any movement (in camera or subject).

You don't need to be a mathematical wizard to be able to convert the standard exposure on the film instruction sheet to a more appropriate set of figures to suit your needs. All you have to do is to set your camera to the recommended standard exposure given for your particular lighting conditions. Having done this, move the shutter speed control until the required shutter speed is in line with the index marks. Note the number of stops you make (eg. 1/60 – 1/125 – 1/125 is two). Then make the same number of stops (eg. *f*11 – *f*8 – *f*5.6) on the aperture ring. On cameras where you can move the two rings together, the correct balance between the lens aperture and the shutter speed is maintained so that the correct lens aperture will automatically line up with your selected shutter speed. More details are given in 'The low-down on camera settings' on page 176.

## Lenses

Most cameras have one fixed lens, chosen by the manufacturer. Some models however, are designed to be used with a number of different lenses which are described as "standard", "telephoto" or "wide-angle" by people in the know. In case you find these words a bit confusing, the following points summarise the general facts about the lenses that are suitable for photographing people.

*Standard or normal lenses* are the ones that are fitted to most cameras. They "see" about the same proportion of the scene as we can inspect without actually moving our head and have a focal length approximately equal to the diagonal of the negative with which they are used. For example, the standard lens for a 35mm camera has a focal length of 45 or 50mm. (The diagonal of the 24 x 36mm negative is 43mm.)

The general features of standard lenses are:

1. They are compact and easy to use
2. They produce crisp, sharp images
3. They are available with fairly wide lens-aperture settings and therefore permit the use of high shutter speeds over a wide range of lighting conditions.

*Long-focus lenses* create bigger images of distant subjects than standard lenses and consequently capture a narrower, more detailed view of things. A typical long-focus lens for a 35mm camera and one which is particularly suitable for photographing people, would have a focal length of 105mm. A telephoto lens is a special compact, lightweight construction of long-focus lens. To all intents and purposes, it does the same job.

The general features of long-focus lenses are:

1. They allow you to stand well back from the subject and yet fill the viewfinder with a bold image
2. Moderately long-focus lenses (up to about 150mm for 35mm cameras) create portrait images with pleasing perspective

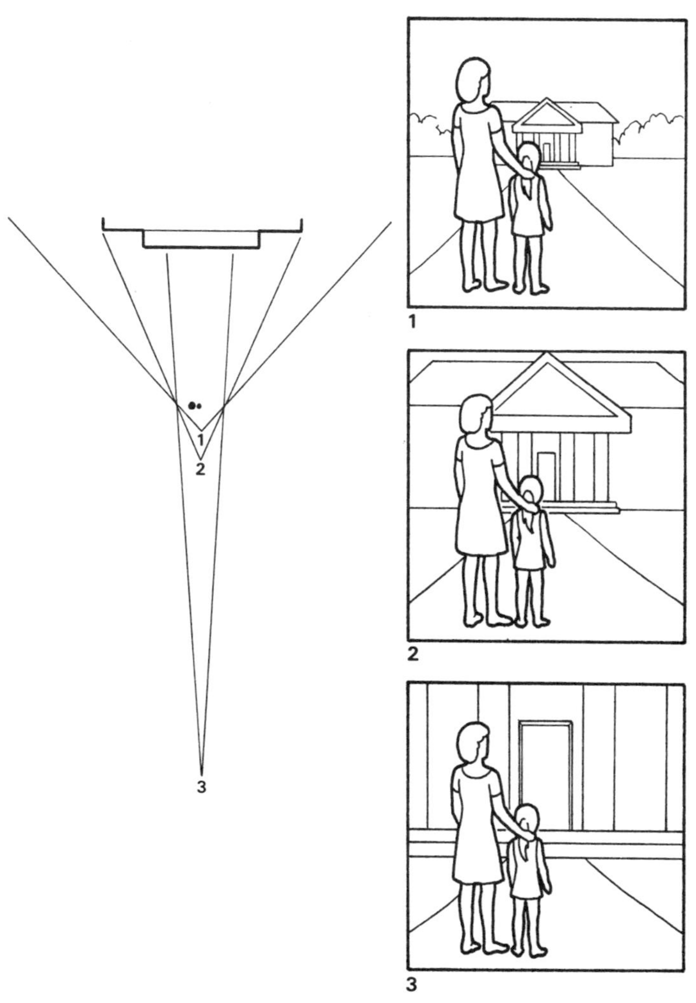


Picture perspective with different lenses. 1. Wide-angle lens at 1m. 2. Standard lens at 2m. 3. Long focal-length lens at 4m.

and enable the photographer to make full use of his artistic skills through selective focusing

3. They magnify movement as well as the subject

4. They do not have such wide apertures as standard lenses and are therefore not so useful for freezing people's movement in action photographs or when the lighting conditions are poor

5. They tend to compress picture perspective

*Wide-angle lenses* have a much shorter focal length than standard lenses and capture a much broader image from a relatively close viewpoint. Popular wide-angle lenses for a 35mm camera are 28mm and 35mm.

The general features of wide-angle lenses are:

1. They allow you to fill the frame with a wide expanse of subject and are therefore ideal for taking pictures in cramped conditions, at receptions and parties for example.

2. They frequently produce pictures with unsual perspective as they image foreground objects disproportionally large in scale to those in the background

3. They create images with considerable depth-of field and therefore can be used to give pictures in which practically the whole subject is sharp (from less than a metre to the far distance)

# How To Take Successful Pictures of People

You will be more likely to take successful pictures of people if you stop and think before you press the shutter. That is much better than simply aiming the camera in the direction of whoever you want to photograph and clicking away in hopeful anticipation that each picture will be a winner. It probably won't. Shooting pictures in a haphazard manner simply leads to disappointing results which over a period can only be discouraging.

A far better approach is to look carefully in the viewfinder each time you frame up on a picture and to ask yourself the following questions:

1. Is the subject interesting?
2. Is the picture arrangement simple?
3. Is the background free of clutter?
4. Does the lighting enhance the picture?

If you can truthfully answer "yes" to each of these questions, you have a successful picture lined up in the viewfinder and should snap it up without delay. It is worth considering some of these points in greater detail since they form the basis of good pictures. (The question of lighting was considered in the previous chapter.)

## Interesting subjects

There is no doubt that some groups of people create greater general interest than others simply because they are more appealing to our emotive instincts. Such subjects can be considered to have good picture potential. Just as some groups of people are more appealing than others, by the same token some situations lend themselves more to photography than others and offer plenty of scope to the photographer.

People in emotional situations also create interesting subjects. The humour of a fleeting incident as the camera catches a joke, the sadness of a mother on her daughter's wedding day or the anger of youngsters involved in a fight – each of these emotions helps to add interest and impact to the situation. It is often easier to achieve successful pictures of people if you select subjects and situations that have built-in picture potential.

Of course, no list is exhaustive, and you are sure to be able to add to this one. It is a good idea to think of your own favourite list of good subjects.

| Subjects with good picture potential | Situations with good picture potential |
|---|---|
| Babies | Children's parties |
| Small children | Weddings |
| Attractive girls | School sports |
| Famous personalities | Carnivals and fairs |
| Weather-beaten characters | Markets and outdoor shows |

## Simple picture arrangments

Successful pictures of people show the subject clearly and simply and are not complicated by irrelevant details. It is therefore a false economy to look at a scene through the camera viewfinder and pack as much detail as possible into the picture area. Such a photograph will contain so much information that it will probably look an untidy jumble with lots of separate happenings competing for attention. A less cluttered view, making a concise statement, will create a far greater impression.

It is often more difficult to create a simple picture arrangement when you are photographing people than it is when you are photographing static subjects like buildings and monuments. The simple reason for this is that you do not have all the time in the world to frame up and shoot when the subject is on the move. Some situations happen so quickly and are so bizzare that you need to work rapidly to snap them up while they last. If you take too long getting your camera up to eye level, or setting the knobs and dials, you will have missed the opportunity to record the incident. The scene will have changed by the time you are ready to press the button.

However, not all pictures of people have to be taken at high speed, more often than not you do have time to take a critical and selective look in the viewfinder before pressing the button. On closer inspection of a particular scene you may decide that the arrangement looks fussy. Frequently a much better view can be obtained simply be standing in a slightly different place to take the picture. It is suprising what a difference a few feet can make.
An effective way of ensuring a simple arrangement is to have the people in the scene filling most of the picture area. To achieve this you can either move in close to take the picture or you can stand at a distance and capture a more intimate view using a long focus lens. However, as most people take pictures on cameras fitted with standard lenses, you will probably be more interested in finding out how to get the shooting distance right with an ordinary camera.

## Get the shooting distance right

When you look at the distance scale on your camera in relation to the person you are photographing, you will discover just how close you need to be to the subject to create a picture that has lots of detail and impact. Generally, it is only by getting in close with your camera that you manage to convey the purpose of a particular picture. For example, perhaps your children and some of their friends are playing "shops" down at the end of the garden and you've been watching the theatricals from the kitchen window. The camera is handy so you take a picture unobtrusively from the back door. When you see the result you can just about distinguish whose children were down the garden that afternoon. You were much too far away to record the detail of the shopping counter and the financial transactions that were taking place, or to capture the intense concentration on the faces of the actors.
Whatever your reason for taking a photograph, the best way to make a clear statment of the occasion is to fill most of the viewfinder frame with a bold close image. The childrens' shop would have made a great picture had the shooting distance been about 2–2.5m (in the region of 8 feet), assuming of course that you were using a normal camera fitted with a standard lens.

The reason why so much emphasis is put on close shooting throughout this book is because most amateur photographers operate at a polite shooting distance when they are photographing people and consequently include far too much superfluous detail in their pictures. If your photographs have suffered from this complaint in the past you can easily help yourself to get the shooting distance right by developing the art of looking at people in the same way that the camera "sees" them.

## Learn to develop a photographic eye

If you want to teach yourself to look at people in much the same way as a camera lens sees them, all you need is time to spare when there are a few people around. You don't actually need a camera. For the experiment find a comfortable park bench or somewhere else where you can sit and relax and watch people moving about. Then you should be all set. Make a rectangular frame with your thumbs and both forefingers before closing one eye. Hold your hands up to your open eye and study the people in the scene before you in your "viewfinder frame". There will be little difference between the picture you are seeing in the frame created by your hands and that which you would see in the camera viewfinder from a similar position (provided the camera were fitted with a standard lens).

In all probability you will find it difficult to concentrate on one particular detail in the scene before you without drawing your thumbs and forefingers together to reduce the field of view. By doing so you will cut out background distractions so that there is a single focal point in the scene that fills most of the remaining area of your viewfinder.

The only way you would be able to create the same uncluttered arrangement in the camera viewfinder is by narrowing the field of view of the camera lens. You could achieve this in two ways. You could either change the camera lens to one of longer focal length which would allow you to maintain the distant viewpoint and perhaps frame up on the scene undetected. Alternatively, there's an easier solution for camera owners who are not geared up with in-

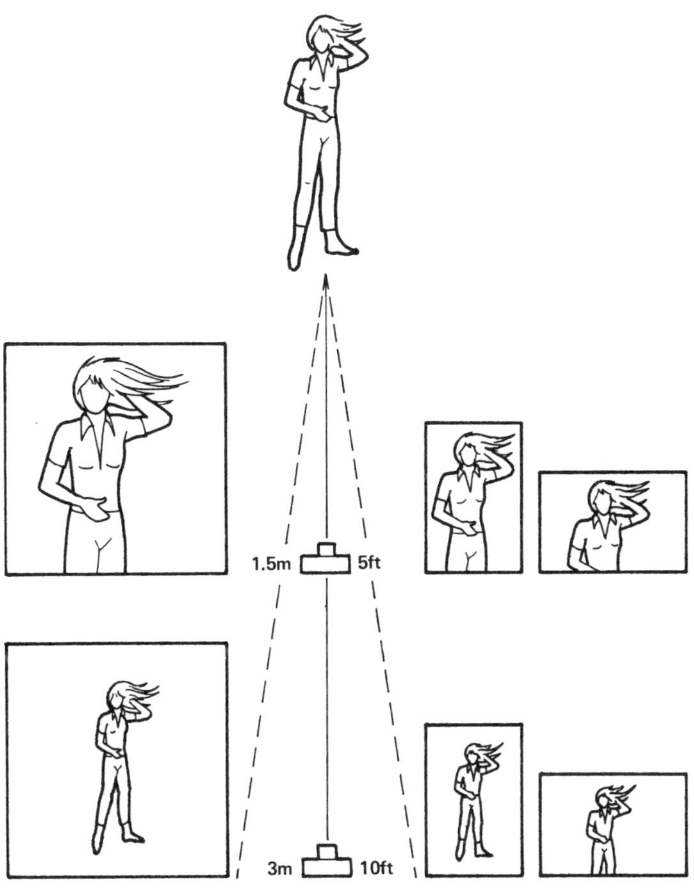


Filling the picture area. The diagram illustrates the size of image that will be formed by a standard camera lens at different camera-to-subject distances on a square format camera (120, 126 etc) as well as on a rectangular one (35mm, 110 etc.)

terchangable lenses, which would be to move in closer to the subject and so present the lens with a more detailed, narrower view. However, there are limits as to how close you can take successful pictures of people. There are two reasons for this, the first is to do with picture sharpness and the second with distortion.

## Picture sharpness close up

Every camera, from the simplest Instamatic to the majestic Hasselblad, has a minimum lens-to-subject distance at which it gives sharp pictures. If the subject is closer than this minimum distance the image will be out of focus and therefore unsharp in the photograph.

The image in the viewfinder of a simple, fixed-focus camera always looks crisp and sharp however close the subject. The best way to avoid getting carried away and moving in too close to the subject is to look up from the viewfinder and to have a quick glance in front of you before taking the picture to see if the shooting distance looks about right. Of course this visual check is only necessary when you are practically within arm's reach of your subject. The minimum camera-to-subject distance is between 90 and 140cm (3–4½ feet) for most cameras of this type. The sharpness problem usually only crops up when you are photographing very small subjects like babies, where you can easily be tempted to get in rather too close just to see the little face clearly in the viewfinder.

If you use a reflex camera or one with a rangefinder, you have a reliable, visual reminder when you are too near to the subject because you will be unable to focus on the scene. When this happens the only way of creating a sharp image in the viewfinder (or superimposing the rangefinder images) is to move back a bit and frame up once again on the subject.

## Distortion

The second reason for not wanting to take the camera too close to people is that your pictures can be spoilt by the unreality of distor-

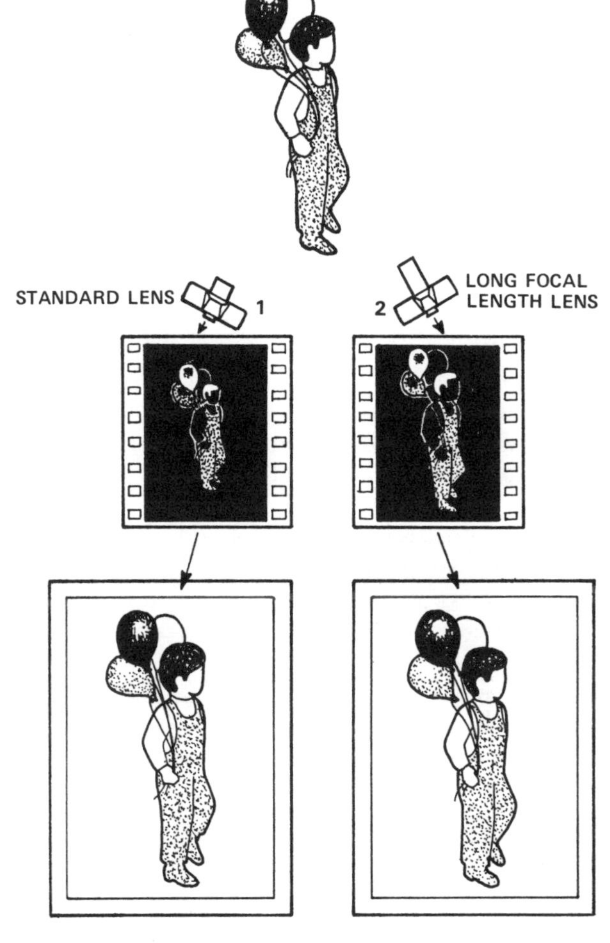


Creating bold images. 1. By enlarging part of the negative area or 2. by filling the frame with a close view to provide a negative that can be enlarged to a greater magnification.

tion. The effect is often called 'wide-angle' distortion, because it is most obvious when you use a wide-angle lens, and so go in very close to your subject.

It's not only the camera lens that sees close objects with a somewhat distorted perspective, the eye does exactly the same thing. You can easily prove this by moving a finger closer and closer to your eye. When you experiment, keep one eye closed and start with your arm stretched out. Move your finger gradually towards the open eye. You will blot out progressively more of the background while your finger appears to get larger and larger as it gets closer to the lens of your eye. You will probably be quite surprised to see a "normal" finger when you take it away from your eye.

Any onlooker might laugh at the scene, but the experiment shows how different things look from a different viewpoint. The trouble is that we are simply not adjusted to seeing things at such close quarters. That is why we find it difficult to accept the distorted, rather exaggerated perspective in pictures taken from too close.

We avoid the discomfort of distortion in real life situations by chatting to our friends at a comfortable conversation distance of around 1.7m (5 or 6 feet). During closer, more intimate conversations we study small areas like the eyes or the lips rather than the entire face. The conversation distance of 1.7m is also the most satisfactory shooting distance for capturing well proportioned pictures of adult faces.

The most frequent reason for distortion spoiling pictures of people is because a hand or a leg moves too close to the camera lens. Perhaps you are taking pictures of the girl friend sitting on the beach, in a side-on view she looks stunning and slim and your pictures will flatter her but if you shoot with her legs coming towards the camera you will convey the opposite effect. Her feet and ankles will appear disproportionately large to the rest of her body. It's easy not to notice this as you are busy focusing the camera. In fact, unless you have a reflex camera, the extent of the effect will not show up in the viewfinder. The easiest way to avoid distortion is to remember to arrange your pictures so that arms and legs and heads that appear in close-up all lie at about the same distance from the camera lens.

The effects of distortion are sometimes used to add impact to pictures. How and why this is done is explained on page 108.

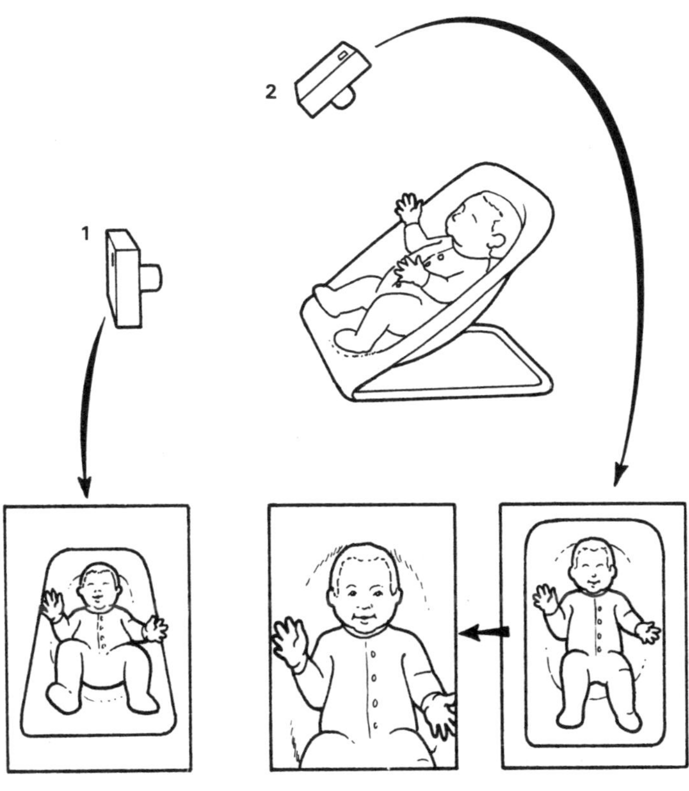


Image distortion in close-up pictures can be minimised by careful choice of camera angle. 1. Unnatural effects obtained when limbs project towards the camera. 2. Well-proportioned image obtained with the camera parallel to the plane of the subject and by enlarging part of the negative.

## Choice of background

A good background for pictures of people is a simple one that enhances the subject. It should compliment the people and not compete with them in terms of texture, colour or contrast. Unsuitable backgrounds contain ugly or obtrusive details which draw attention away from the focal point of the picture – the person you have photographed. There are several techniques you can use to create suitable backgrounds for pictures of people out of the most ordinary settings.

Your choice depends to a certain extent on the type of camera you use, on whether it has focusing facilities as well as an adjustable lens and on whether it can accept other lenses.

The easiest way of getting rid of a problem background is to view the subject from a relatively low angle. This will mean bending down slightly to take the picture and pointing the camera upwards so that you isolate at least part of the subject against the sky. Such a viewpoint gives a much cleaner picture arrangement than the conventional eye level shot taken at standing height. A low shooting angle can be used with any camera for most outdoor pictures of people. The obvious exceptions are when you are shooting in a really built-up area or in a crowded situation like a market place.

Another simple solution to the problem of cluttered backgrounds is to move in close with your camera so that the people you are photographing fill most of the picture area. There will be little room left for background distractions to appear in the picture. In addition, the shot will benefit from the added impact afforded by the close view. This is another technique that can be used with any camera.

If your camera has an adjustable, wide aperture lens it is relatively easy to separate the subject from an obtrusive background by controlling the relative sharpness of the image areas so that the subject stands out in perfectly sharp focus against a blurred background. You can not, of course, camouflage all background distractions, particularly when you are shooting on colour film. The out-of-focus image of a bright red pillar box, for example, will appear in your pictures as an even more garish red blob and no amount of focusing control will reduce the intensity of the colour. In this case, you just have to choose a different viewpoint.

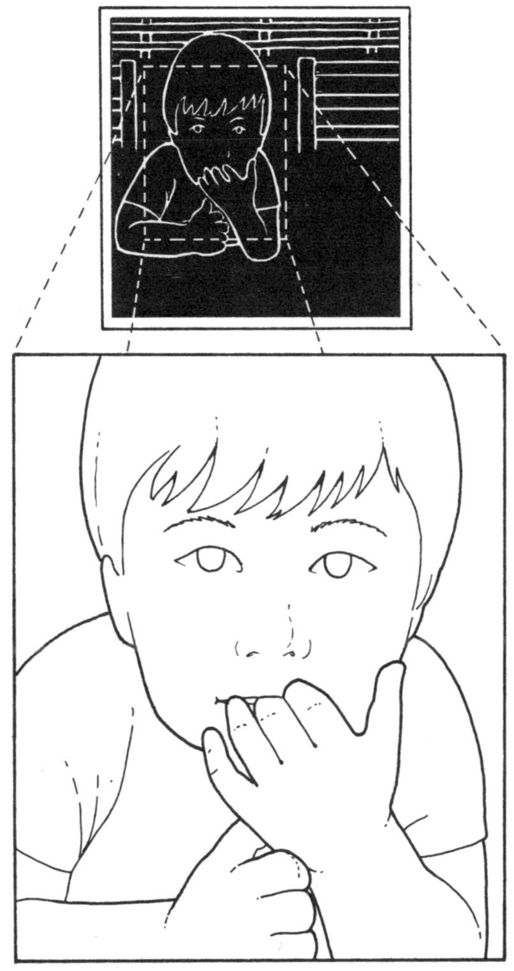

Picture composition can often be improved by enlarging part of the image area. In this selective enlargement the background distractions that were recorded on the negative no longer spoil the image.

## Controlling picture sharpness

When you are photographing people with an adjustable, focusing camera you instinctively focus the lens on the most important part of the subject. This will be a prominent figure in a group of people, a baby's head in a Christening shot or a child's eyes in a close portrait. Having done this you can vary the degree of sharpness in each picture by adjusting the aperture setting. By selecting a large lens aperture (for example, *f*3.5 or *f*2.8) much of the picture will be out of focus and only the region around the point on which the camera was focused will appear sharp in the picture.
Conversely, with a small lens aperture for example, *f*11 or *f*16, some of the subject in front of the focusing point and most of it behind will come out in sharp focus. The actual amount of control you have over picture sharpness depends upon several factors. The greatest differential comes if you use a long focal length lens at its maximum aperture from close to your main subject. The further your subject is from the background, the more blurred will become the background. Being able to control the zone sharpness is a great advantage when you are photographing people because it allows you to create artistic pictures in the most unlikely situations. You can tone down the distraction of fussy background or foreground details simply by moving in close to the subject and shooting with a large lens aperture.
Suppose you are taking pictures at a school fete. There are lots of people around and you've got the camera focused on a small boy sitting nearby on the grass with an ice cream in one hand and a goldfish in a jam jar in the other. The situation has all the makings of a super picture if it were not for the background which is a jumble of arms and legs and handbags. It's an impossible situation to photograph well on a simple camera but with an adjustable model all you need to do is to set the aperture to its widest opening to throw the background out-of-focus. By doing so the emphasis of the picture is concentrated on the boy and his winnings. You can easily create just the right effect simply by setting the camera lens to *f*2.8 and adjusting the shutter speed by an equivalent amount to maintain a well balanced exposure.
If you want to make certain of over-all pin sharp pictures you have to

increase the zone of sharpness to cover the entire picture area. For this to happen you'll need to set the camera lens to a small aperture and to keep the subject at a reasonable distance from the camera. The technical term used to describe the distance in the subject which can be imaged in sharp focus by the lens is depth-of-field. There's more about this in the technical tips on page 180.

### Records help progress

If you are just starting to concentrate on photographing people, quite a good approach is to record relevant details of exposure and shooting conditions as you shoot each frame on a film. Then, when your film has been processed, you can compare the facts and figures you have recorded with the resulting pictures. For example:

AUGUST SHOOTING BLACK-AND-WHITE FILM (ASA/BS 125)

| Frame number | Subject | Weather conditions | Exposure | Camera-to-subject distance |
|---|---|---|---|---|
| 1 | Old man | Bright sun | 1/250 *f*11 | 4.5m 15 feet |
| 2 | Man with pipe | Cloudy dull | 1/125 *f*5.6 | 1.5m 5 feet |
| 3 | Children on swing | Cloudy bright | 1/125 *f*8 | 1.75m 6 feet |
| 4 | Child laughing | Bright sun | 1/125 *f*11 | 1.75m 6 feet |

When you first glance through your pictures you will doubtless be pleased with quite a few of them. They will probably be the ones that showed people in natural situations, the children with grubby knees and faces; a girl friend with the wind in her hair smiling happily; or mum, duster in hand, sporting her weekday pinnie.

The best shots will be those which are correctly exposed – although if you've really caught a winning expression, or the emotion of the moment, you'll not notice if the picture is a fraction too light or a shade too dark as your attention will be held by the impact of the image. If you are not satisfied with any of the shots you will find that your notes will provide clues as to what went wrong. Having established the faults, the task of correcting them shouldn't be too difficult.

A summary of the comments on the previous shots might read as follows:

COMMENTS SHEET

| FRAME NUMBER | SUBJECT | COMMENTS | NEXT TIME REMEMBER TO: |
|---|---|---|---|
| 1 | Old man | Too much background in picture, figure much too small | Move in closer with camera – 2.5m is a good shooting distance for a full-length figure |
| 2 | Old man with pipe | Closer view has much more impact – would have been perfect had more of the picture been in focus | Select a camera angle that images the pipe and the hand holding it at roughly the same distance from the camera to avoid distortion |
| 3 | Children on swing | Picture surround is sharp but the child and the swing are very blurred | Shoot at 1/500 sec. to freeze rapidly moving subjects at a distance of 3m |
| 4 | Child laughing | Natural picture with impact – lighting rather contrasty | Manoeuvre things so that the subject is back-lit. Adjust camera exposure by 2 stops* |

* That means giving an exposure of 1/250 second @ *f*5.6 in a similar situation.

Before you take your next roll of film have another look at your previous efforts. Chances are that you will see additional good and bad points which you will either want to emulate or improve upon the second time round. And when you have completed another film keep up the good work of analysing your results, for the more you look at pictures, other people's besides your own, the better you will become at taking them.

## Composition

When you start exploring photography a bit more deeply you are bound to come across the topic of photo composition. It's the subject of several complete books, a favorite for magazine articles and is usually of great concern to the judges of photographic competitions. Composition is a theoretical explanation of why good pictures are good. The explanations came into being because artists and photographers studied successful pictures and tried to identify all the separate design elements that gave the pictures their appeal. Things such as colour, shape, line, tone and form were considered in relation to the unity of the picture and their effect on the balance and impact of the result.

Picture composition is a subject that is worth reading up when you are starting to take creative pictures. You will find it useful to apply a few of the rules to your own picture taking situations before you begin to develop a style of your own. However, after a while, you will discover that really eye-catching pictures have something more than just good composition, they have that extra bit of creative flare that makes them come to life and make a clear statement in the strongest possible way.

Among the elements that contribute to a well composed picture are:

. Simplicity of subject arrangement and the shapes and forms within the picture.

. Contrasts such as those between colours, light and shade, textures or the size of objects. Chosen correctly, they can add interest and vitality to the subject of the picture.

. Patterns which, when repeated, help to create unity.

. Balance so that the distribution of colours, tones and shapes creates an even, artistically pleasing effect.

. A strong focal point, which gives the picture a prime centre of interest.

. Perspective, which can be suggested by the size of different objects or by receding lines.

To get an idea of how these elements of composition can be related to your own pictures of people, have a look at some of your successful shots to see if the subject is:

1. Positioned in a commanding part of the picture area
2. The focal point inside a natural frame
3. The most colourful or the brightest element in the picture
4. The area of the picture in sharpest focus

If you have said "yes" to a couple of these points you are probably already looking at people in a critical way and selecting the best camera angle and lighting to create a feeling of reality and unity in your pictures. If not, you may be able to pick up some tips if the ideas are explained more fully.

## Subject position

When you are looking in the camera viewfinder there are usually one hundred and one different positions in which you could place the subject. Some are obviously better than others and it has been established from successful photographs that you are more likely to be pleased with the result when the main point of interest lies slightly off centre, in fact along lines that divide the picture into approximate thirds. You've only got to think of something like a passport photograph where everything is dead centre, symmetrical and boring to realise the importance of subject placement.

## Natural frames

Foreground frames to pictures of people help to create an illusion of depth by making the viewer look into the picture towards the subject. The frame can be anything that's conveniently nearer to the camera than the people you are photographing – doorways, flowers, windows, trees, fences, bridges or arches. The illusion of depth is heightened if the frame is darker than the subject.

When you are photographing people in crowded situations you can

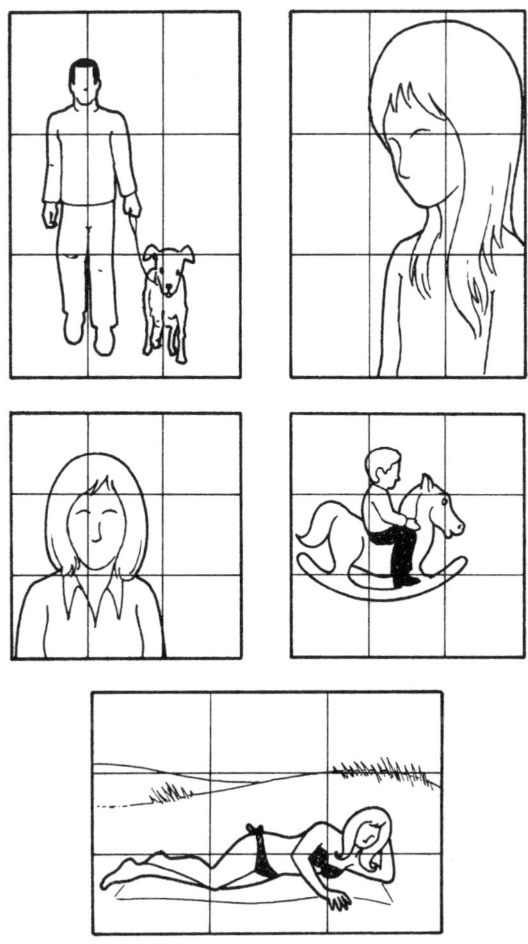

Examples of subject placement to show how the compositional strength of a picture is heightened by positioning the most important area of the image along lines that divide the picture into approximate thirds.

often obscure unwanted, fussy details by carefully choosing a foreground frame to block out offending clutter. The frame doesn't have to completely surround the subject, nor does it have to be symmetrical. A suitable frame should blend with the mood of the subject.
If the frame is closer to the camera than the minimum camera-to-subject distance for sharp pictures, it will appear unsharp in the photograph. This is usually quite acceptable provided it doesn't dominate the picture.

## Colour

Colour is an important element in picture composition because the mixing and positioning of different areas of colour within a photograph can affect the success of the result. Reds, yellows and oranges are definitely eye-catching colours whereas browns and purples merge well with the surroundings. The impact created by bright colours is much greater when they are confined to the small area of a photograph. Consequently, if bright splashes of colour appear on the edge of the picture area, as a blur in the background or as an indistinct shape in the foreground, they will probably attract as much if not more attention than the people in the picture.
Another aspect of colour which applies particularly when you are photographing people is that of clothing colour clashes. When you are out taking candid shots you don't usually get the opportunity to arrange things to perfection but, when you are photographing the children or formal happenings, it pays to be a bit more careful. The bride and groom will not be too happy to compete for attention with two clashing red dresses standing next to each other in the group pictures. If you are directing operations it's a simple matter to arrange the ladies so that they are well apart, preferably on opposite sides of the wedding couple.
You often hear people talk of colours as warm or cold. Warm colours are red, yellow, orange and brown; and cool ones are blue, green and mauve. In general it's advantageous to picture composition to keep the cooler colours in the background and the warmer ones in the foreground since, by doing so, you can emphasise the feeling of

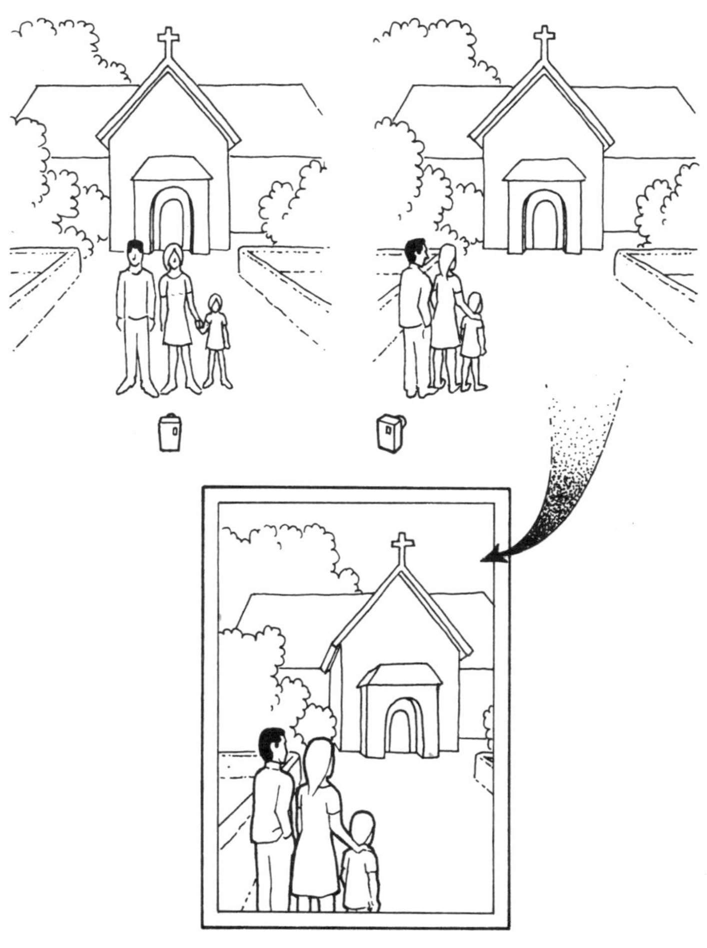

The diagrams show how picture perspective can be increased simply by selecting an angled view of a scene and by having the family inspecting rather than the camera.

depth in the picture. Cool colours compliment a subject whereas warm colours and strong contrasts create an impression of activity and interest.

For the final word on colour it is worth remembering that some of the very best colour photographs are almost colourless. So when you are taking pictures of pink-faced babies or rosy-cheeked children the high key approach can be very effective. High-key pictures are those in which the subject is softly lit and the image is one of lightness and delicacy created with the help of white or lightly-coloured clothing and a white background.

# Photographing Babies

Babies are undoubtedly the most photographable and the most photographed subjects around. From the moment of birth, camera shutters start clicking to provide pictures for the parents and the grandparents as well as the aunts and uncles. Once an infant loses that tiny-baby-look and begins to take an interest in the outside world it will have universal camera appeal. Pictures of babies crop up in many places: they are used extensively by the media to symbolize just about everything that is pure, clean and honest; they are prominent among the prints in photographic displays; they adorn the windows of nearly every photographic studio and, quite naturally, they are to be found in practically every home in the country.

## A new baby?

The prospect of a new baby in the family is frequently the cause of a renewed interest in photography. If you are the expectant parent as well as the photographer don't rush out and buy a new camera if you already have one. You don't need an up-to-date, black-finished model for taking pictures during the first few months. Why? Because you are going to be far too preoccupied with other things when baby actually arrives on the scene to bother about the technicalities of a new camera. Your days will be fully taken up with four hourly feeding, extra washing and catching up on sleep. In between the baby routine you'll be entertaining friends and relatives who are bound to want to call to see the latest addition.

Once life with the new baby settles down to a regular, unflustered pattern you will have time to learn the ins and outs of a new camera and to experiment with it. Meanwhile, stick to the camera you know so that you can take pictures easily without spending too much energy or time on it; you'll have no surplus of either for a few weeks. Since tiny babies are relatively static subjects, even the sedate, reliable Box Brownie could, if dusted, be used for taking pictures during the first couple of months. They do, however produce rather small pictures, because you must stay well back.

If you are having your first baby you have probably read all the pre-natal literature that is available and also browsed through a number of baby magazines. You might well imagine that a brand new baby has a chubby smiling face and a clear smooth skin. Pictures without captions can be misleading because newly born babies are seldom chubby and are unable to smile. Advertisers frequently use "established" babies to promote their merchandise because new born babies are not particularly photogenic at close range. On top of that, they are rather small as well as a bit floppy and are therefore not the easiest of subjects to photograph attractively. Fortunately your pictures of baby don't have to have universal appeal, they simply need to tell a very precious story which will bring back happy memories in years to come. Every baby is a different little person and to see your own baby grow and develop is one of the great fascinations of life. As no two children are alike it is impossible to say when you will be able to expect a particular stage of development to be reached. For this reason you should keep your camera handy so that you can frame up quickly when baby discovers a new trick and looks extra appealing and savour the memory in a photograph.

## Making a baby book

There is a pretty good chance that you will be presented with a baby book the moment your friends hear about the new arrival. Besides containing pages on which you can enter the relevant weights and measurements, there will be lots of space for you to fill with pictures. (For details of making up an album see pages 202–204.)

During the baby's first few months try and keep the album as up-to-date as possible. If you stick in the pictures and caption them as you go along you will be able to remember the sequence of events that the shots cover. To add variety to the pictures in your album include a few enlargements of your best shots and trim those that contain untidy and irrelevant details. Trimming pictures has the added advantage of introducing a selection of unusual formats to the somewhat regimented enprints that feature in so many baby books and photographic albums. A combination of square, horizontal and vertical formats of varying dimensions will certainly enhance the overall impact of the pictures in your baby book.

## At the beginning

There is no better place to start a story than at the beginning: the birth. As the proud new father you may be able to take a few shots shortly after the birth. This might be frowned on in some hospitals but it is amazing how unobtrusive you can be if you have determination. A little pocket-sized camera is really an asset on such an occasion as it can be kept tucked away out of sight right up until the moment you want to take a photograph. Even though you will need to use a flash bulb to light up the scene, the whole job should only take a second or two.

Visiting hours are not the best times for photography as the wards are bustling with activity and commotion. It is far better, if the hospital permits photography, for mum to keep a camera in the bedside locker so that it is handy during the day when things are a bit more relaxed. You will probably have already been told that anything left in a locker is there at your own risk so this is not the place to leave a camera that you really value.

Besides taking pictures of your own baby you may chum up with another mum who will be delighted to be presented with a shot of her and her offspring. Some hospitals keep the babies in cribs that are made of clear plastic so that baby can be easily seen and photographed from lots of different angles. You will want to get in close with the camera as there will not be very much of the baby on view as it is enveloped in wraps and blankets. Have the camera at the ready when baby is weighed. If you miss the first weighing session, ask the nurse when the next one is due so that you can be ready to snap up a picture at an opportune moment.

One of the rewards of having a baby is being spoilt with cards and flowers. The cards, of course, can be reserved along with other mementos but, sadly, the flowers soon fade, particularly in a hot hospital atmosphere. If you are inundated with beautiful blooms you will certainly want to take a picture of the display before you leave.

Probably you will do most of your photography towards the end of your stay in hospital. Even if you only manage a few informal shots of scenes in the ward the results will be well worth the effort; you cannot decide to do it later.

During a home confinement there will be a hundred and one things to think about besides photography. if you think you might like to take a few pictures it is wise to buy the film and load it into the camera well in advance of the event. Keep the photographic gear in the bedroom so that you are not rushing around looking for things at the last moment.

In the first few weeks photography will have to fit in with the baby routine. Frequently a good time to take pictures is after the 10 a.m. or 6 p.m. feed for even a new-born baby usually follows these feeds with an alert spell. As baby gets older, so the waking spells become longer and the photographic situation becomes more flexible.

PHOTOGRAPHIC POSSIBILITIES WITH A NEW BABY

| Event | Possible photographs |
|---|---|
| Bath time | 1. Medium distance shot of mother holding baby in the baby bath |
| | 2. Close-up of soaping operations |
| | 3. Medium shot of baby swaddled in towels |
| | 4. Close up of a clean dressed baby snug in mother's arms |
| Morning play | 1. Long shot of the pram in the garden (perhaps taken from an upstairs window) |
| | 2. Medium shot of mother looking at baby |
| | 3. Close up of baby lying in pram |
| Lunch | 1. Medium shot of mother preparing the bottle |
| | 2. Close up of baby drinking from |
| | 3. Medium shot of 'bringing up wind'. |

The first baby is quite an experience for everyone involved. All the things you will be doing will be new and different, so you will probably want to take quite a few pictures to tell the story. The chronicle will be more interesting if it contains a variety of pictures, long shots as well as close ups, single shots of fleeting moments as well as picture series containing two or three shots to describe an event in detail.

If you are about to photograph a friend's baby and are not used to handling such a small bundle you may not have developed the firm holding technique that assures baby that all is well. When you are uncertain what to do, leave the lifting and shifting to the parents as any uncertain approaches may upset the peace.

## Problems and solutions

An average baby is about 50cm (about 20 inches) from top to toe at birth which makes it a pretty small subject for photography. In fact, if you have never studied a tiny baby through a camera viewfinder you may not have realised just how close you need to be to get a detailed view. For example, even if you go as close as you can with fixed-focus camera, the image of a fully stretched baby from top to toe is unlikely to fill the viewfinder area completely. Using the standard lens on a focusing camera you may do slightly better, the focusing will allow you to move in closer so that baby will just about fill the picture area. Even then, you are unlikely to be able to produce a full-frame picture of baby's face.

Since you are dealing with such a small subject in the early weeks of photography, your first baby pictures will show quite a bit of the surrounding scene. Because of this you will want to be careful to select camera angles that present the most attractive and straightforward view. That is not too difficult with such an immobile subject, as there will be plenty of time for you to look carefully at the picture in the viewfinder and move around a bit with the camera before actually taking the picture. When you do have to contort yourself to get a good view of the baby, in the bath or the bassinet for example, it might be possible to move things into an open space on the floor while you take a few photographs.

In fact, the floor is usually a pretty safe place for a young baby. It is the favourite position for shooting the more formal, Christening-type pictures where both baby and the clothes can be arranged attractively without harm coming to the infant. To make the presentation as simple as possible spread a white blanket or shawl over the carpet, particularly if it is a patterned one, and lay the baby down on it. The white surroundings will not only help to create a neat unpretentious picture, they will also reflect light onto the subject and so give you a softer, more attractive portrait. Try shooting from a high angle so that the camera is looking down onto baby. Taken from this angle the picture will contain all baby and blanket and no background clutter and will therefore have a single centre of interest – the child.

As we have said, babies cannot hold themselves in a pose, they need to be supported. Make sure that the support does not clutter or confuse the picture. A good idea for shooting mother-and-baby pictures is to have the baby wrapped in a shawl so that his back and head can be supported by out-spread hands underneath the shawl. The drape of the shawl will hide the angular distraction that might otherwise spoil the softness of the photograph. The best time to shoot is when mum moves her head near to baby so that their two heads are almost touching. If the scene looks stiff and posed try shooting again later when baby is due for a few cuddles and kisses.

## Lighting

Photographs of the baby during the first few weeks will, in all probability, mostly be taken indoors where it is warm in the winter and relatively cool during a long hot summer. This will mean using either flash or a fast film and available light. The brief light from electronic flash or flashbulbs does not harm a baby's eyes.

If you have a simple camera or one with only a few adjustments on it you will certainly need to use flash for indoor pictures. Follow the advice given on page 116. With such a very small subject you need to take particular care to resist the temptation of getting in too close with the camera and flash, otherwise your pictures will be overexposed (pale and lacking in detail). Of course, with a suitably small

lens aperture, or a "computer" flash this is no problem.
When you are shooting by available light you will be able to take full advantage of the diffused nature of window lighting. Exactly how to do this is described on page 191.
For picture taking outdoors you want the lighting to be soft and diffused, which it will be in the shady spots in which you position the pram for the baby's afternoon nap. If the shade is being provided by a nearby tree like a birch or an oak, it will probably be dappled as the sun will filter through the large open network of branches. This type of shade lighting is not quite so suitable for photography as the dense, even shade that is provided by solid objects and thick foliage.

## Three to six months

At about three months photography becomes much more rewarding, and in some ways easier too. Your subject is no longer immobile and tiny; he has become alert and animated as well as stronger and longer. Although you will not be chasing around after him you will certainly need to have your wits about you when you move in close with your camera. A bigger baby will fill a bit more of the picture area and leave less vacant space to be filled with the surrounding scene. If you continue shooting with a camera-to-subject of around 1.5m (5 feet) your shots will gradually begin to feature the baby more prominently and his antics and expressions will create the focal point in your pictures.
Now is the time to bring out noisy and diversion-creating toys to attract baby's attention and turn on the smiles. Be ready to take pictures the moment you shake the rattle or crinkle the cellophane to attract his attention. A young baby is unable to sustain enthusiasm for very long and if you have to fumble with the camera you may miss the chance to shoot a good picture.
At this early stage it helps if both mum and dad are involved with the picture taking, one "working" the camera and the other the baby. Once the baby has decided he wants to play and be the centre of interest, his attention and his gaze will focus on the toy that is being used to amuse him. If the diversion is taking place in the direction of the camera, the picture will show the baby looking into the camera

lens. If you press the button on cue you should manage to capture a picture of an excited expression and animated arms and legs.

## Picture taking opportunities

Between three and six months many of your pictures will probably show the baby lying down or sitting supported by cushions as he will still be unable to sit by himself at this age. Brightly coloured cushions create a busy background and draw attention away from the subject. If you have control over the picture taking situation choose props that are white or plain pastel colours so that the baby forms the focal point of the picture.

The modern little bouncing chairs are great for picture taking as they are easy to position for photography without any fuss or bother. Provided the baby is used to sitting in the chair he will be quite content to perform for the camera in a choice spot. The position should be well-lit from the photographic point of view, a shady place in the garden is ideal. A fairly high viewpoint generally gives the most satisfactory results at close camera-to-subject distances. (See diagram on page 39.)

At about this age another good photographic angle is achieved by laying the baby on his tummy and shooting with the camera level with his eyes as he pushes himself up on his arms to get a better view of the world. Different backgrounds, shooting distances and camera angles will produce different pictorial effects. For example, with the camera just above ground level, nearby objects such as table and chair legs will appear large and menacing. This effect is emphasised in a side-on view as more of the background detail appears in the photograph. A simpler, softer picture arrangement can be created by taking a front view of baby's head and arms. If you can focus the camera on baby's eyes and take the picture using the widest possible aperture, the background detail including baby's feet, will be blurred and out of focus in the photograph.

For a more formal, studio effect, try laying baby down in the centre of a large bed. It should be possible, by carefully selecting your camera angle, to take pictures with baby surrounded by the bed cover but without including any background furniture at all. If you shoot against a plain bed cover or a white or pastel coloured sheet the picture will have all the simplicity of a studio portrait. It is best to have two people on the job just in case the baby tries to roll off the bed.

Taking photographs from low down is a problem if your camera has only an eye-level viewfinder. For some, you can get a right-angle attachment to enable you to look down into the eyepiece. If you intend to concentrate on baby photography, though, a camera with a "waist-level" viewfinder – with or without an eye-level alternative is a better proposition.

Besides photographing every-day events to keep the baby album up-to-date, you will want to record some of the humorous happenings that occur. Possibilities for picture series include:

| Event | | Possible photographs |
|---|---|---|
| Feeding time | 1. | Medium distance shot of baby in baby chair (choose a picture-taking spot with a simple uncluttered background) |
| | 2. | Long shot of mother presenting the cereal bowl. |
| | 3. | Close-up of baby's face as he takes his first gulp. |
| Visiting grandparents | 1. | Long shot of baby with grandparents. |
| | 2. | Close-up of baby inspecting grandma's present. |
| | 3. | Medium distance shot of grandma and grandchild. |
| Baby friends | 1. | Long shot of friends arriving with all their paraphernalia. |
| | 2. | Medium shot of the babies surrounded by their toys. |
| | 3. | Low angle close-up of babies playing together. |
| Out walking | 1. | Long shot of mum or dad pushing the pram (A side-on view is usually best). |
| | 2. | Close-up of baby sitting in state. |

If you have a baby bouncer hanging in a doorway you'll be able to capture some lively expressions as baby jogs about. To add variety to your baby story take a few unusual shots, perhaps, if you have some close-up equipment, a close-up of baby's hand or foot; a shot of the washing line full of baby clothes; a picture of the baby's collection of toys or teddy bears.

## Six months to a year

Once the baby has gained a bit of muscle power and confidence there will be no stopping him. Within an amazingly short space of time he will learn to sit up and then to crawl and probably before his first birthday he will be careering about in a baby walker, chasing phantom figures around the house and out into the garden. He will be wearing his first proper pair of shoes and gradually losing his baby looks.

Photography can have its ups and downs during this period as teething can cause quite a few off days which no one in the family will want to remember. However, if you escape these traumas you will find that practically every day something new and exciting happens; cupboards and drawers will be pulled open and the contents examined, the telephone will attract a great deal of attention and no stone will be left unturned in the garden. Your belongings will mysteriously appear and disappear as they are discovered, examined and discarded; for baby's life is full of new and fascinating things and the latest discovery is always more attractive and fascinating than the previous one.

Keep on the look-out for humorous situations as the child becomes more adventurous. If you miss an incident the first time round, the chances are it will happen again as most babies take a delight in showing off their latest feats.

Many youngsters spend as much, if not more time playing with household objects as they do with their own toys. A couple of cotton reels, an empty carton, a ring of keys and a purse form a good collection to keep a baby occupied for quite a while. Once you have provided the bait all you need to do is to watch and wait. When the situation warrants a picture, get in close with your camera so that the baby fills most of the area inside the viewfinder frame and shoot quickly because the baby's actions and expressions are beginning to change more rapidly now.

As you are likely to have your hands full with everyday affairs, keep your camera handy and set, more-or-less ready for quick shots – focused on $2\frac{1}{2}$m (8 feet) and with a suitable aperture and shutter speed for conditions at the time.

If you are able to take close up pictures you may fancy celebrating the arrival of your baby's first tooth with a photograph to mark the occasion. This is one of those shots that are easier to take with two people on the job, one with the camera and the other coaxing a wide smile at just the right moment. It will need to be quite a chuckle for you to get a good view of the emerging incisor. As the first tooth is usually in the bottom jaw you will get a better view if you shoot from a fairly high camera angle. An alert young baby will quite naturally want to investigate the shiny black object that is so tantalizingly placed in front of him. You will need to be prepared to move the camera quickly out of reach if you want to avoid collecting sticky finger marks on the lens.

It is quite a good plan, if friends arrive with their children for an afternoon in the garden, for you to keep your camera on view. The obvious advantage of this is that it is immediately available for picture taking whenever you might want to snap up a situation. In addition, your activities are less likely to attract attention once everyone has become used to seeing the camera around. You can not expect a picture situation to remain "just so" as you dash indoors in search of the camera; for competent crawlers will simply stop what they are doing and follow you indoors to join in the fun.

As picture-taking opportunities increase you can afford to be more discriminating about those you choose to photograph. You will be able to be a bit more fussy as to the suitability of the lighting and the background. You can afford to wait for really impact-creating situations before getting trigger-happy with your camera. Once you are able to become more critical of the photographic potential of a might even start to win you a few prizes in competitions.

## The first birthday

The big event at the end of the baby's first year is the first birthday party. And, although this is not usually such an energetic affair as those of later years, it is nevertheless an important landmark which will probably be celebrated with the Grandparents and a few young friends and their mums.

At the start of the party you will want to photography the presents and the babies seated on the floor, eyeing each other as well as the new toys. Then there will be the birthday tea. It is worthwhile taking a quick picture of the laden table before the guests arrive – things will probably be a bit chaotic and disorderly with so many small mouths to feed and the attractive display of goodies will suffer in the turmoil.

Detailed studies of the birthday child gazing at the candle on the cake and close ups of the other youngsters' faces as they get covered in food while sampling the delights of wobbly jellies and cold ice cream will have far more impact than more distant shots. Besides, a table surrounded by an assortment of high and low chairs and their occupants is not a very easy subject for photography from an overall viewpoint. For suggestions of lighting and camera angles to use at birthday parties, see pages 112–114.

An effective way of recording the passing years is to plan to take a picture of the baby in the same spot on each birthday. You will need to choose a suitable position, either in the house or in the garden which will be just as good for a picture of a baby as it would be for a shot of a fully grown teenager. You may decide to take a sequence of pictures with the child posed near a garden seat or a favorite piece of furniture so that in later years the seat or the bookcase or the hall stand can be lent on rather than stood beside. Furniture or fireplaces are ideal for gauging the annual increase in height.

The pleasure that a picture record of this sort will give you in later years makes the effort of creating it seem quite insignificant.

**Other people's babies**

Many photographers find it easier to take formal portrait-type pictures of other people's babies than they do of their own, particularly once the crawling stage is reached and the infant becomes more independent. The main reason for this is that the parents are usually on the scene to lend a helping hand. They will be only too happy to coax a few chuckles and cute expressions out of their off-spring to provide the photographer with an abundance of camera potential. The situation usually calls for close-up studies for which diffused lighting is ideal. A high-speed fllm is preferable for outdoor photography so that fast shutter speeds can be used to capture the spontenaity of the moment. Indoors, the most appropriate lighting is bounced or umbrella flash (for details of both see pages 183–185).

# Photographing Young People

Once the first few hesitant steps have been accomplished you will have no end of fun watching your baby's antics. If you had the time and the film to spare you could spend hours taking pictures of his activities as he learns to do all sorts of photogenic things. Incidents like climbing on his bike, pushing his wheelbarrow down the garden or sitting himself down in his own fireside chair all spring to mind. Each acvitity is accomplished with great deliberation and an enormous amount of concentration, so much so that the brief click of your camera shutter will pass unnoticed.

A toddler's moods and expressions change from one minute to the next as he becomes delighted, exasperated or just plain bored with whatever he's doing. You'll have plenty of opportunities for photographing humorous situations as he studies his picture book upside down, or chases a fleeing bird with a crust of bread. You will be able to capture scenes of provocation as he stands on tiptoe to reach up high for tempting objects on shelves and table tops. And when he's bored and fed up, that's the time to catch him sitting motionless, wistful and wide-eyed oblivious of the dribble as he debates what to do next.

## Planning

Few so-called candid shots of toddlers are complete chance. Of course you cannot force a smile or a cute expression, neither can you make a toddler perform against his will, but you can assist the situation. You can put the toys, the paddling pool or the baby swing out in the garden in a shaded spot and then be in ready with your camera, watching and waiting for things to happen.

Another solution is to put the child into something like an attractive basket or a large washing up bowl and to take as many close up pictures as possible before he realises how to escape. Whenever you set up a situation though, have a helper close by, just out of view of the camera, to prevent the baby tipping backwards and hurting himself.

When your toddler is fully mobile you will need to summon all your powers of patience to cope with some of the exasperating things that are bound to hinder your photographic efforts. There will be times when you are all focused and framed-up on a terrific picture just waiting for a slightly better expression or for the child to look up for a fraction of a second, then suddenly, without warning, before you have a chance to press the shutter, he's rushed off and left you looking sheepishly at the camera. Alternatively, perhaps you are all ready to shoot a close up and the child will lunge forward to give you an affectionate hug just as you hear the shutter in motion. In spite of the feelings of exasperation and frustration you are bound to have from time to time as you attempt to photograph your offspring you will find that the pre-school years are the best for photography. You will see more humorous happenings and cute expressions as the infant acquires new skills and plays inventive games with young friends during this stage of his development than at any other.

## Shoot from a low angle

When your toddler is resting on his haunches contemplating his next adventure you might fancy taking some shots with the camera actually on the ground. However, when the camera is right down low you need to be careful that the lens has an unobstructed view of the scene. Nearby stones and tufts of grass will appear as featureless blobs in a photograph and not as the attractive foreground frame that they appeared to be in the viewfinder. To reduce the amount of foreground in such a picture all you need to do is to point the camera upwards slightly. This shooting position is particularly effective when you can isolate the subject against a background of sky.

Parents get into the habit of stooping down and bending to talk and play with their young children, so it is quite natural for them to take pictures at a low level. However, if you are not used to youngsters it's worth reminding yourself before you start using your camera just how small even the toughest little toddler actually is. Bend down beside him and study the scene from his level – it is quite frightening to see the size of things from down there.

## Pictures outdoors

Outdoor activities are much easier to photograph successfully than most of those that take place indoors. There, the restrictions imposed by crowded conditions and the limitations of simple flash lighting make creative, natural results difficult to achieve. Outside, you can concentrate on picture-making. As young children seldom stay still for more than a moment, most of your outdoor pictures will be taken while the child is in motion. Perhaps he will be running, jumping, skipping or simply fidgeting about contemplating what to do next. Different photographic techniques are required to record successful pictures of, for example, children running flat out to those used to capture shots of them when they are merely ambling along killing time.

For photographic purposes, childrens' actions can be divided into those that take place fairly close to the camera and those that take place some distance away. The difference between the two is the relative effect they have on image sharpness. the direction of movement, whether it is away from or towards the camera or across the field of view, and its speed also affects the sharpness of the image. It is possible to heighten the effects of movement by blurring the image or to strengthen the impact of an achievement simply by selecting an appropriate camera technique.

## Movement

Artistically blurred pictures are great for conveying a child's vitality and have terrific impact when seen enlarged in photographic displays. However, shots of your children, particularly those that are taken with a simple camera which are destined for the family album and are therefore unlikely to be enlarged beyond the enprint stage, are better for being clear and sharp.

## PHOTOGRAPHIC POSSIBILITIES WITH YOUR TODDLERS PLAYING OUTDOORS

| Event | | Possible photographs |
|---|---|---|
| In the sandpit. | 1. | Long shot of the child sitting in the sand surrounded by buckets and spades. |
| | 2. | Close-up of the serious business of turning out a sandcastle. |
| | 3. | Close-up of the child's laughing face. |
| | 4. | Medium shot of the afternoon's work. |
| Action on the roundabouts. | 1. | Medium shot of the child being helped onto the see-saw. |
| | 2. | Close-up of the child sitting in state. |
| | 3. | Low-angle shot looking upwards as the see-saw rises to its highest point. |
| Helping in the garden. | 1. | Medium shot of toddler and father digging in the vegetable garden. |
| | 2. | Close-up of the youngster inspecting a worm. |
| | 3. | Close-ukp of the fence with an inquisitive robin looking at the scene. |
| | 4. | Medium shot of the workers returning with their produce. |
| Cowboys and Indians with older brothers and sisters. | 1. | Medium shot of the actors dressed up in their war paint and plumage. |
| | 2. | Close-up of an Indian in hiding. |
| | 3. | Medium shot of a Cowboy giving chase on his bicycle. |
| | 4. | Medium shot of the parties negotiating a peace plan. |

To make certain of capturing a reasonably sharp image of a moving subject with a simple camera it is advisable to:

1. Take pictures in bright sunshine
2. Choose a shooting angle that images the child moving towards or away from the camera
3. Take the picture when the movement is sedate rather than hectic
4. Keep the subject a fair distance from the camera.

Actions taking place near the camera, especially when the child is rushing around and moving across the picture, are most likely to cause blur. A slightly blurred image of an active child can be quite effective particularly if the camera angle has been selected to include foreground objects in sharp focus. A low angle is ideal if you want to include such things as a tricycle or a scooter in the foreground with the child in the middle distance against a background of clear sky.

If you want to record sharp pictures of the ever-changing, rapid movements of children at play, out on the sports field or simply letting off steam in the back garden, you will need a fast shutter to freeze the action the split second it is recorded by the camera. The diagram gives you an idea of the approximate shutter speeds required to freeze the movement of a youngster on a bicycle. More detailed information on coping with subject movement is given in the sporting section of the chapter "Photographing People Out-and-About", pages 93–97.

Toddlers playing will provide you with some great opportunities for taking interesting picture series. The sort of occasions for which the descriptive treatment is suitable are shown on the following table. In all these examples it is the action that makes the picture interesting, and, because the toddlers are occupied, both their pose and expressions are relaxed and natural. the fact that the hair is untidy, the face a bit dirty and the clothes rather crumpled adds a touch of reality to the situation.

## Pictures indoors

The most convenient way of documenting indoor happenings for the family album is by taking flash-on-camera pictures of the

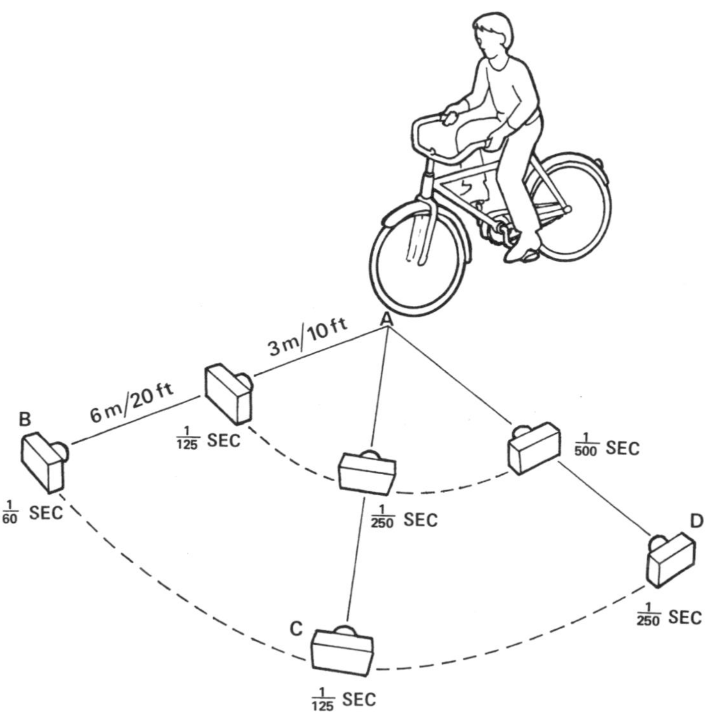


Freezing movement. Approximate shutter speeds required to freeze movement at different camera positions: AB movement coming towards the camera; AC at 45°; AD at right angles, across the field of view. Position B is the idea spot for shooting movement on a simple camera.

daily routine. Young children seem to delight in helping with the household chores, brushing up, dusting, washing. Whatever mother's doing, it is likely her youngsters will be close by lending a helping hand. When they use the wrong equipment for the job or struggle with adult-sized implements you ought to be able to get some very amusing pictures, provided the camera is handy and loaded with film.

Picture possibilities at Christmas and other festivities are legion. So many new and exciting things happen. While Santa Claus remains a real and trusted friend you will want to photograph the scribbled note as it is sent up the chimney, and the bulging stocking hanging at the end of the bed. On Christmas day you will be taking pictures as the presents are being opened. Then there are the gifts being handed down from the Christmas tree, as well as photographs of the children playing with their new toys and the serving of the Christmas lunch. These are only a few of the happenings you will want to photograph during the festive season. You will probably need to lay on extra supplies to ensure that you do not run out of film or flash while the shops are shut.

If you are interested in creative photography you will want to experiment with more versatile forms of lighting than flash-on-camera.

## Photography at the play group

A play group is the ideal place for taking candid shots of young children together. If your child attends a local group, the organisers may allow you to visit one morning to photograph the children and their various activities. This is not something that you can do in a hurry as it will take a little while for the children to get used to you and return to more serious things like painting and listening to songs and stories. You will need to take plenty of film and be prepared to mooch around and watch and wait for photographs to happen.

## Bigger and bigger

As children get bigger they become more sociable and their play becomes more adventurous and boisterous. There will be plenty of opportunities for good photography around the home as well as when you go out at weekends and on holiday. The sort of situations that create good picture possibilities are:

| Pictures in the garden | Pictures indoors |
|---|---|
| Playing with the garden hose | Dressing up |
| Splashing about in the paddling pool | Playing with mother's make-up |
| Building houses | Practising carpentry |
| Playing shops | Painting |
| Building a snowman and snowball fights | Playing with model railways |

As the years pass you will find that the school and weekend activities youngsters engage in such as music, dancing, horse riding and sports begin to occupy them more and more. All too soon childhood happenings will be just a memory and dates and discotheques will be the order of the day.

## Other people's children

If you like being with young children and have a great deal of patience you will probably find the challenge of photographing your friends' children an extremely satisfying and rewarding outlet for your photographic talents.

Discovering the likes and dislikes of different children is one of the fascinating aspects of child photography. Each child you meet is a different little individual with his own characteristic mannerisms. Some children are chatty and friendly with cheerful grins and infectious laughs; whereas others are shy and reserved with wistful eyes and thoughtful expressions. Fortunately, most children make no bones about their feelings and you can get to know them quite quickly.

Once you are on friendly terms with a toddler it's a relatively simple matter to photograph him at play, particularly when he is outside pottering about with his toys in the garden. If you have mastered the basic photographic techniques of exposure and lighting and are able to compose a pleasing picture, you are bound to be successful.

## Informal portraits

You can, of course, pay special attention to portraying a child's particular characteristics in your pictures. This really comes within the realms of portraiture because you will need to concentrate on photographing facial details to capture fleeting expressions and typical mannerisms. To do this you have to get closer to your subject than you do to photograph the usual informal pictures of play situations. Close to, the region of accurate image sharpness must be carefully chosen and accurately positioned if you are to obtain really successful results. Consequently, it is essential that you use a camera that has fully adjustable focusing for your portrait photography.

The conventional area of sharp focus in child portraits is the eyes. They are the most expressive feature and are usually quite large in proportion to the rest of the face. In fact to be strictly accurate, as you will want your focusing to be, it is the boundary line between the coloured iris and the contrasting white surround that is generally selected.

It's not easy to focus accurately and at the same time to capture the child in a natural attitude with an unaffected, spontaneous expression. You will soon discover this when you try photographing a toddler's face for the first time. Even when a child is sitting down his legs and arms are usually darting all over the place and each animated facial expression coincides with a toss or turn of the head. If you watch the child's face and then reach for the camera and start focusing when a typical expression appears you'll despair of ever capturing natural portraits.

The next time you are taking pictures of a friend's toddler try carrying on a normal chatty conversation as you are using your camera. Then, at the same time, carefully watch the image in the viewfinder rather than the child's face. While you are talking, constantly adjust the camera focusing so that the eyes are sharp all the time. You will see the child's expression change as the conversation progresses and when a particularly happy smile beams through the viewfinder you can fire the shutter with confidence, knowing that the image will be sharp.

Children who have grown up with a camera around the house will probably never suffer from camera nerves and will be totally untroubled about being photographed. However, not all children are quite so blasé and you will doubtless come across some who find it difficult to behave naturally in front of strangers. Without reassurance they are unable to ignore something as persistently intrusive as a camera, particularly one held so close to them by someone of whom they are not quite sure.

Fortunately such children are in the minority. They can usually be photographed successfully if you are prepared to spend quite a bit of time paving the way for your photographic efforts. A reserved, preschool child will probably feel more secure if mum or dady were to stick around and will gradually become less self-conscious as you chatter away. Ask questions about this and that, the name of a friend or a favourite doll, the make of a toy car or what they had for lunch or tea yesterday. Bend, sit, kneel or even lie down so that you can converse at the child's level, rather than at an awe-inspiring adult height.

If possible arrange to take the pictures in the child's home rather than your own because children are usually more relaxed in familiar surroundings. It's often a good idea to be discreet about your camera gear and for neither the parents nor you to mention photography until you have got to know the child. If there is any fussing or special clothes the youngster will immediately be on guard and your chances of fun and good picture taking will diminish rapidly with every action.

## Lighting for informal portraits

When you start taking informal portraits you will be much more successful if you use your camera outside rather than indoors in the sitting room or the child's bedroom. That's because you will be able

to select an area that is well lit for photography and manoeuvre the action into that area. If you stay indoors you will have to grapple with furniture and flash. These are unnecessary complications when you want to concentrate on mastering new focusing techniques.
The most satisfactory lighting for child portraiture is soft, totally diffused daylight. That is the sort of lighting you get on a cloudy day or when it's sunny but hazy. On a bright sunny day the lighting will be soft in areas that are shaded from the direct sunlight. Soft lighting accentuates facial details and texture and gives a natural effect which is just what you want in an informal portrait.
When you are taking portraits outdoors on an overcast day, or when you are shooting them in open shade, you will get slightly better results with colour films if you use a skylight filter over the camera lens. The filter absorbs ultra-violet radiation which, although invisible to the human eye, registers as blue on the film. There is often quite a lot of ultra-violet about in the shaded lighting that is best for informal portraits. So, unfiltered colour pictures tend to have a slight blue tinge. The skylight filter, which is slightly pinkish, has a beneficial warming effect when used with both colour print and colour slide films. It has no effect on exposure.

## A portrait session

A good approach to an afternoon's photography outing is to take a packet of crisps or a tube of chocolate beans along to help break the ice when you first arrive on the scene. Then you can really start to get to know the child while having a cup of coffee and a friendly chat with the parents. Children like to take part in adult conversations, they frequently butt in with an impatient nudge or an "excuse me" and then forget what it was they wanted to say or jumble up their words in the rush to get them all said while they have your attention. Once you've been accepted as a friend you'll probably be invited to take a closer look at their toys and possessions. This is a good time to begin to think about broaching the subject of photography. Your actual approach will obviously depend on the situation, but quite a good introduction is to offer to photograph a favourite toy. Intelligent three or four-year-olds will be most impressed if you explain about lighting and camera angles and will be very willing to assist. When you have established a working relationship with a child you are well on the way to creating the right situations to take some good portrait pictures.

The secret of success is not to rush things. When you are photographing the tractor or the teddy bear, encourage the child to look at the image in the viewfinder – sharing the experience is part of the game. At this stage if the camera is on a tripod your efforts will seem doubly impressive. When children discover that taking pictures of toys is fun they will probably demand to have their own picture taken in order to prolong the game. You will want to remove the camera from the tripod so explain that you will need to follow their every movement with the camera in order to take pictures that both of you will like. You cannot over stress the point that is is a joint effort, even a three-year-old will understand enough to want to be involved in the picture-taking. It's most important for any future relationship that you do not forget to give them their own picture of their favourite toy as promised. Of course if someone in the family has a camera that produces instant pictures this would be an ideal opportunity for using it.

Another good game is to pretend that being photographed is all a big secret and that mummy and daddy want to surprise grandma and grandpa with a very special present. Children like surprises and having secrets and will probably be only too happy to help you.

There are two traps that you can unwittingly set for yourself, both of which can make the going rather hard. The first is to specifically ask whether or not John or Jane actually want to have their picture taken. The straight answer will almost certainly be "no". Toddlers are very honest and rarely want to do things they don't fully understand. The second trap that you want to avoid is to issue seemingly irrelevant requests like "say cheese" or "watch the birdie". Such comments can easily break the tempo of the photography game for the logical reply to them is "why?" and then you'll be stuck for an adequate answer.

When you have finished taking pictures, continue playing and chatting for a while. If you break off suddenly the child will think that the whole effort was a try on for the camera and will feel less inclined to co-operate in the future.

## Children and their pets

Children of all ages love to play with animals and the addition of a new kitten or small puppy to the family will provide you with endless hours of amusement and many good studies for photography. Young animals are easiest to photograph when they are weary from rushing around and ready for some gentle play. To create successful pictures you will need to move in close with your camera as both puppies and kittens are quite small subjects compared to a three or four-year-old.

## The early school years

Once the serious business of learning the three R's begins and the children settle in at primary school, your record photography for the album will be confined mainly to weekends and school holidays. You will want to use your camera on family outings to places like the zoo and the seaside and to capture the fund of summer picnics and country rambles. There will be plenty of opportunities for you to take pictures of school activities during open days, at the Christmas carol concert or nativity play and at the summer sports or swimming gala. Whatever the occasion, you will want to capture close ups of the children being themselves and medium shots of their activities. If you set your camera to a fast shutter speed you will find it easy to record happy faces and the wild gestures of boisterous children having fun. You will need to anticipate actions and expressions to take successful pictures of moving subjects on a simple camera. (Details of how to do this are given on page 66).

When you are taking more formal portrait shots you will find that many of the tips given on pages 74–5 still apply although you will need to be prepared for a more adult line of chatter as you pave the way for each picture. Don't be surprised if you get asked some pretty searching questions about what you are doing and your equipment. If you can supply interesting and informative answers to these, you may well be sowing the seeds for a future interest in photography.

## Photographing 8-to-12 year-olds

Once at school, children soon get into the routine of things. As they begin to widen their circle of friends and start to follow new pastimes they will spend progressively less and less time around the home. When there are no extra lessons to attend, their leisure hours will probably be occupied with clubs or group activities, bicycles, plastic modelling or hobbies that take them out-and-about discovering things. If you can keep up with their ever-changing fads and fancies you should still be able to find opportunities for using your camera to record pictures for the family album.

Many children go through an athletic spell around this age as they learn to master the skills of different sports at school. You will probably find your own kids only too willing to pose in front of your camera dressed-up in uniform colours when they win a coverted place in a school team. But it is out on the sports fields that the real action takes place and that's where the best pictures are to be had. For tips on how to photograph action see pages 98–102.

## Young teenagers

It is not unusual for teenage children, even those from the most photographically-orientated families, to become gawky and diffident in front of a camera as they grapple with the problems of puberty. Many young teenagers are only too happy to loose themselves in a loud dreamworld of pop music and discotheques to escape from the realities of growing up. It may be diplomatic to forget about taking close-up portrait pictures and to be more discreet about photography for a while. There will be ample opportunity for family pictures, to keep the album up-to-date, when you are all together away on holiday or enjoying a rest in the garden in the cool of a hot summer's evening.

It is often in their early teens that youngsters begin to want to stand behind the camera instead of in front. Perhaps they will be requiring pictorial records for projects or learning about the hobby at the youth club or school camera club or even studying the subject for school examinations – whatever the reason for their interest, your experience and encouragement will be of great value.

## Photographing girls

There has never been a better time for photographing girls. With our modern attractive fashions and natural-looking make up, there are great opportunities for really good photography. There are three different methods of approach. Either you can take candid pictures when you are out-and-about with your camera, alternatively you can photograph girl-friends in picturesque settings outdoors, directing operations when necessary, or you can go in for the more formal indoor sessions for which you need to direct the model and control the lighting.

## The candid approach

If you are keen on the candid approach then it is worth going some place where you know there will be plenty of people and action as well as lots of attractive girls. Why not start looking for talent at local sporting events; not only will you probably be able to spot some good camera material, you will also find photography easy as your subjects will be fully occupied watching the sport.
There is no doubt that some girls enjoy being photographed and others don't, and those who are totally unaccustomed to cameras and photographers frequently stiffen up awkwardly at the mere thought of having their picture taken. That is where the candid approach scores because if you see a super-looking subject who obviously enjoys life and having fun, you needn't give her a chance to freeze up if you are unobtrusive about your shooting. That is easy to do if you keep your distance and rely on your equipment to provide you with a forceful close-up of the girl. If you do not have a telephoto lens, distant shooting will give you an over-all view of the scene and you will have to enlarge a small part of the negative to get the same close-up as you would with a long lens. When the degree of

enlargement is going to be considerable, your results will be more satisfactory if you:

1. Shoot the picture on a slow or medium speed film so that the image grain in the enlargement does not adversely affect picture sharpness
2. Use a fast shutter speed so that the negative is completely free from camera shake and the image well defined
3. **Are especially careful with camera focusing. Make sure that the negative you use to make the enlargement is pin sharp. You can check for sharpness by inspecting the negative with a magnifying glass. (If you check image sharpness take care not to touch the image area of the negative with your fingers because creasy marks will show up on the print)**

## The girl-friend or boy-friend

Your enthusiasm about photography is bound to rub off on any regular friend. You can reinforce that if you get into the habit of using him or her as a model in some of your pictures. Because you know each other well your model has probably got into the habit of relaxing in front of the camera and adopting easy-looking positions when you are about to shoot. If you are using your friend in scenic shots to add interest to the view, have the friend looking at the scene and not straight at the camera. Experiment with different lighting effects, try taking silhouettes at sunrise and sunset (see page 110 for details on photographing silhouettes) and soft-lit head-and-shoulder shots against natural backgrounds such as bracken, wild flowers, tree trunks or the sky.

While you are shooting, try to keep a look-out for small details that may spoil the effect of the result like underwear straps showing on the shoulders or a badly turned collar or polo neck. When you feel the urge to throw in a few words of direction, try to be constructive and precise about what you say. Continue chatting about this and that inbetween asking for a shoulder to be turned towards the camera or a chin to be raised a little.

If you get too serious about the whole business you will find it difficult to create spontaneous, happy pictures. An effective technique is to invent some action for your partner to do. A toss or turn of the head, a twist towards the camera or a request to remove a wisp of hair from the face will divert attention away from the camera lens. Then, if you take the shot the moment the action ends, you should catch a relaxed and natural pose.

If you find it difficult to explain the effect you are trying to create or the attitude you want your friend to adopt, a quick demonstration usually does the trick. And, if this doesn't work, don't labour the point, try a different idea or move on to another location because as soon as either of you begins to get fed up with things the situation and consequently your pictures will lose their spontaneity.

As you are working you may have vague impressions at the back of your mind of the glamorous studies of beautiful girls and their debonair escorts in way out fashions that you've seen in Vogue and other such glossy magazines. There is no reason why you should not be able to create pictures just as attractive, particularly if you choose photogenic settings to work in. The sort of places that inspire enthusiasm and creative efforts are:

The landscaped gardens of palatial houses

Grand old buildings with attractive courtyards and balconies

Glass-houses full of exotic plants and palms

Apple orchards in the spring

The woods in autumn

Botanic gardens in the summer . . . etc.

Wherever you choose to take your friend and your camera you need to work the setting itself into your pictures so that there is harmony between the model and the surroundings. You can do this by shooting through close-up foliage and close to nearby masonry so that your model becomes part of the scene. The foreground and background will give extra dimensions to the picture. The relative importance of these elements can be subdued by the use of selective focusing so that the attention of the picture is centred on the sharpest area which should be your model. To be successful with selective focusing you need to focus the camera lens carefully and to shoot with a fairly wide lens aperture (*f*5.6 or *f*4 for example).

Even with a simple camera you can still soften the effects of the surroundings by using one of two special techniques. The first is to

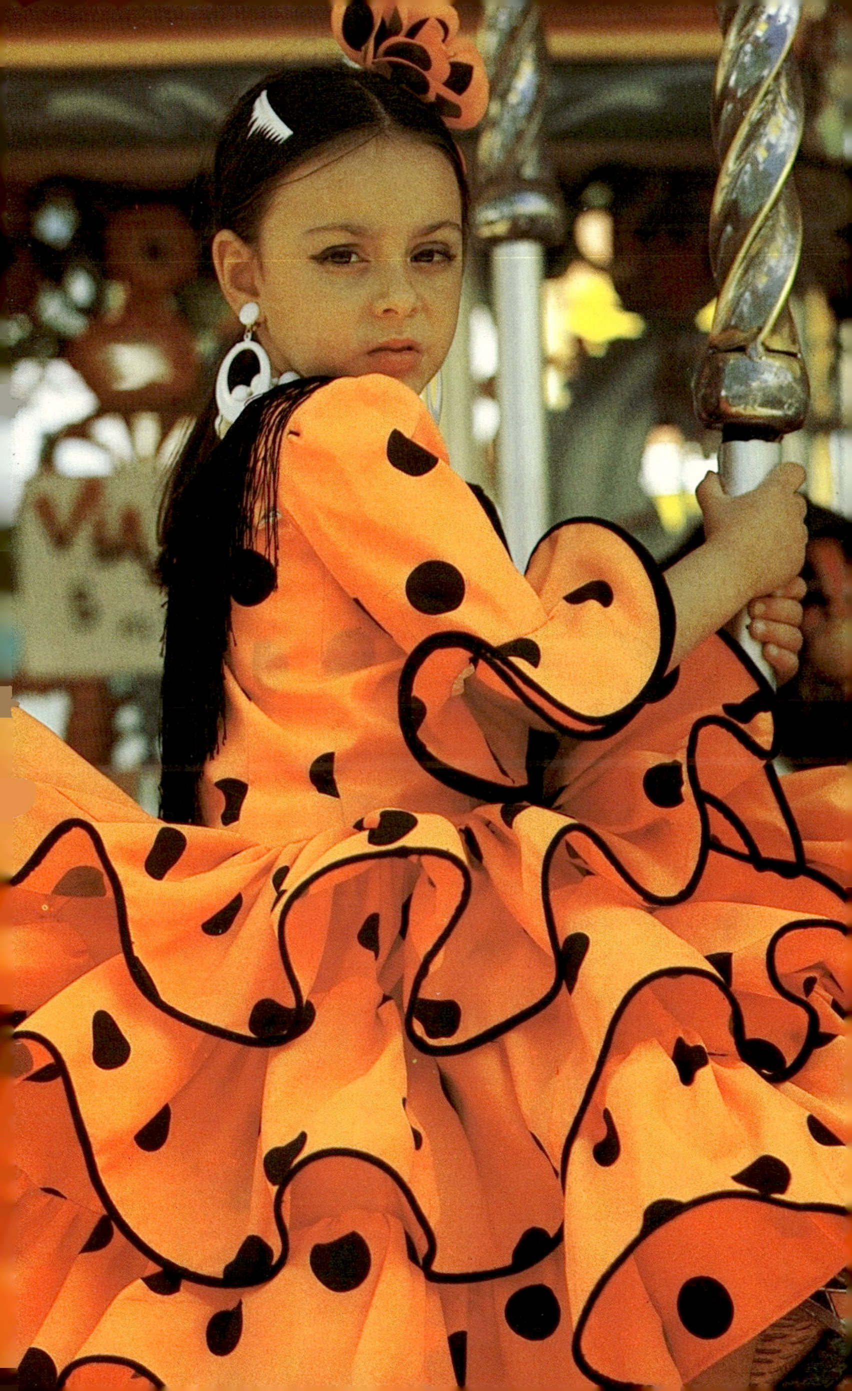

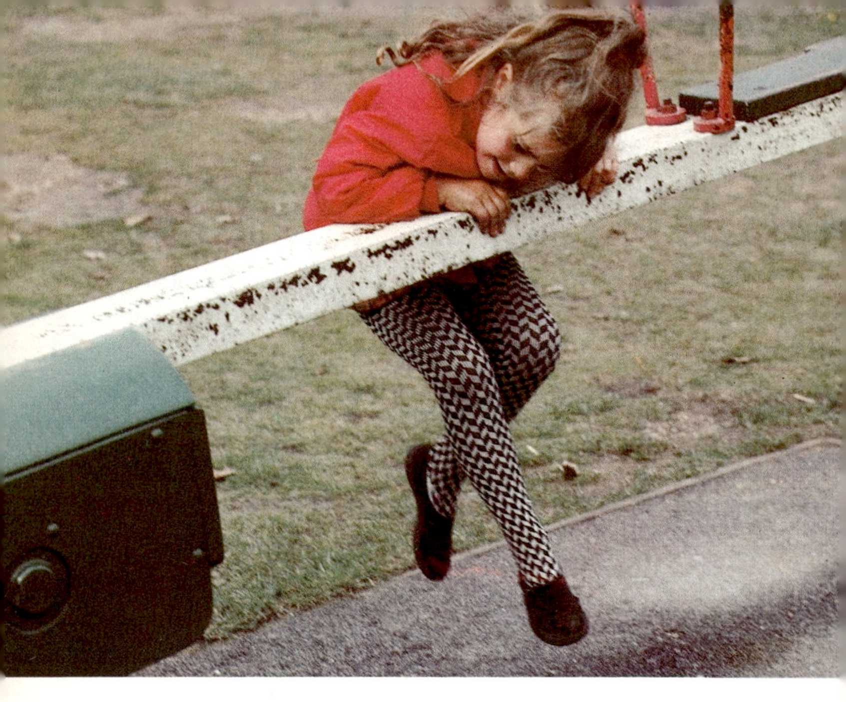

Record a situation in more than one way. These two pictures from a series complement each other – *Alison Trapmore.*

*Page 81.* People doing things are always an attraction. This little girl dressed for the feria makes a colourful picture – *Jeff Marion.*

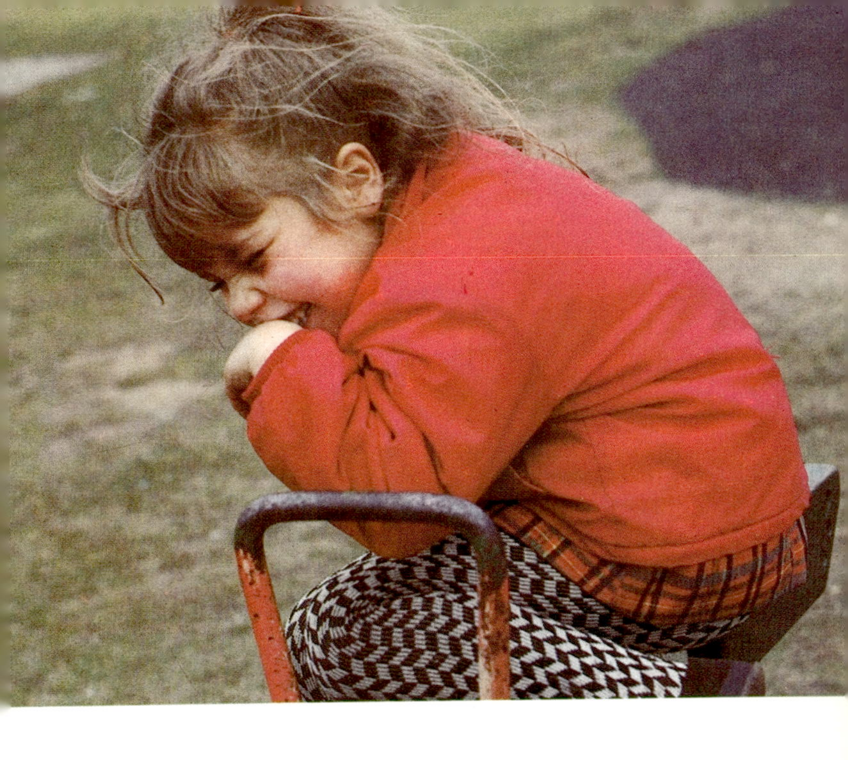

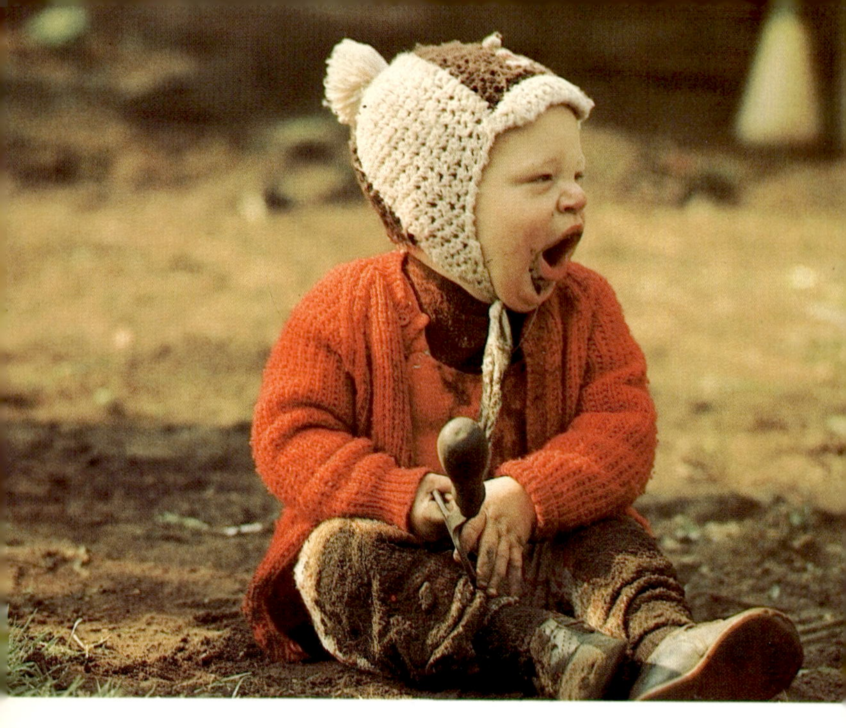

Don't restrict your photography to the clean, prepared occasions. Pictures of children playing their own games often have a natural charm. Hazy sun provides soft attractive lighting – *Alison Trapmore.*

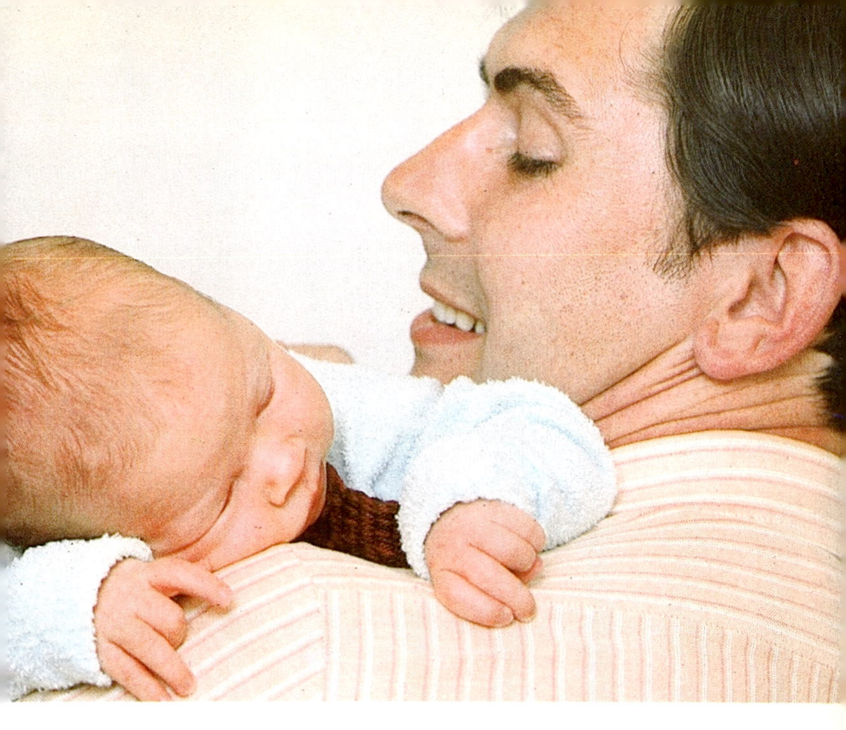

The size of young babies makes them difficult to pose with adults. Try to put them nearer the camera, as here, with father virtually forming a frame – *Alison Trapmore.*

*Page 86, 87:* Look for situations where the lighting can simplify your composition. Whether it be shade to give a virtual silhouette, or the spotlight effect of the sun through the trees – *Mary O'Neill, Alison Trapmore.*

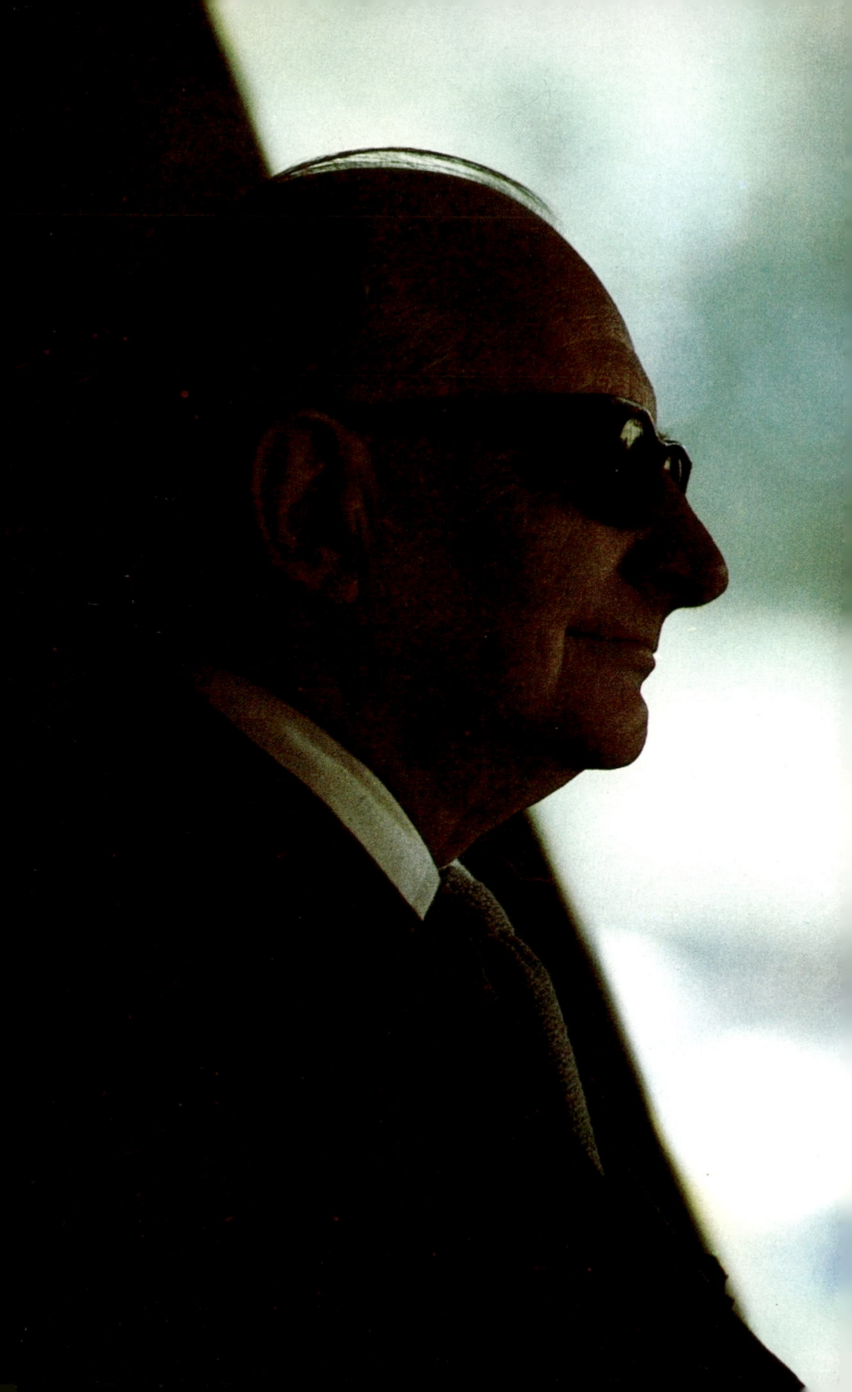

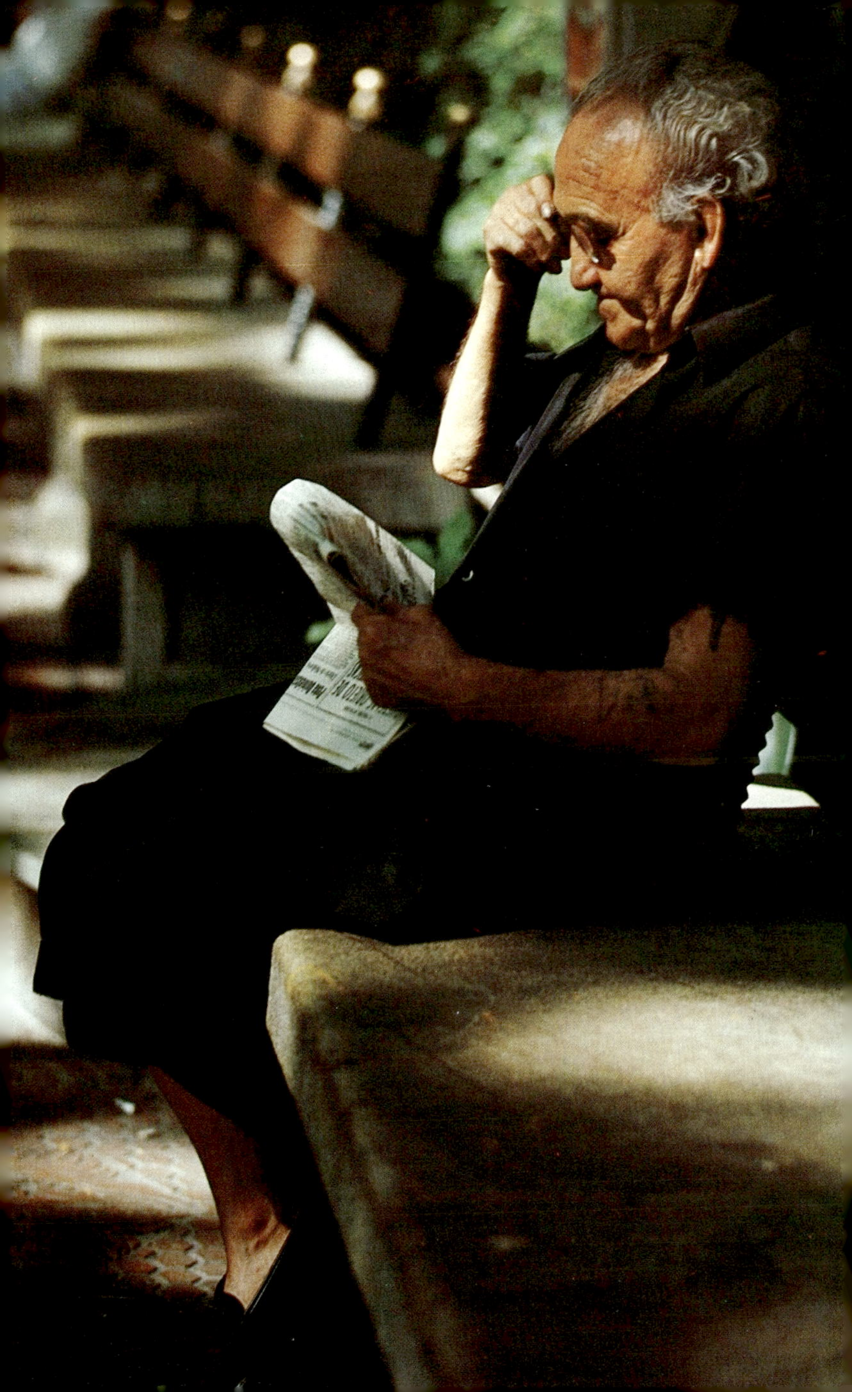

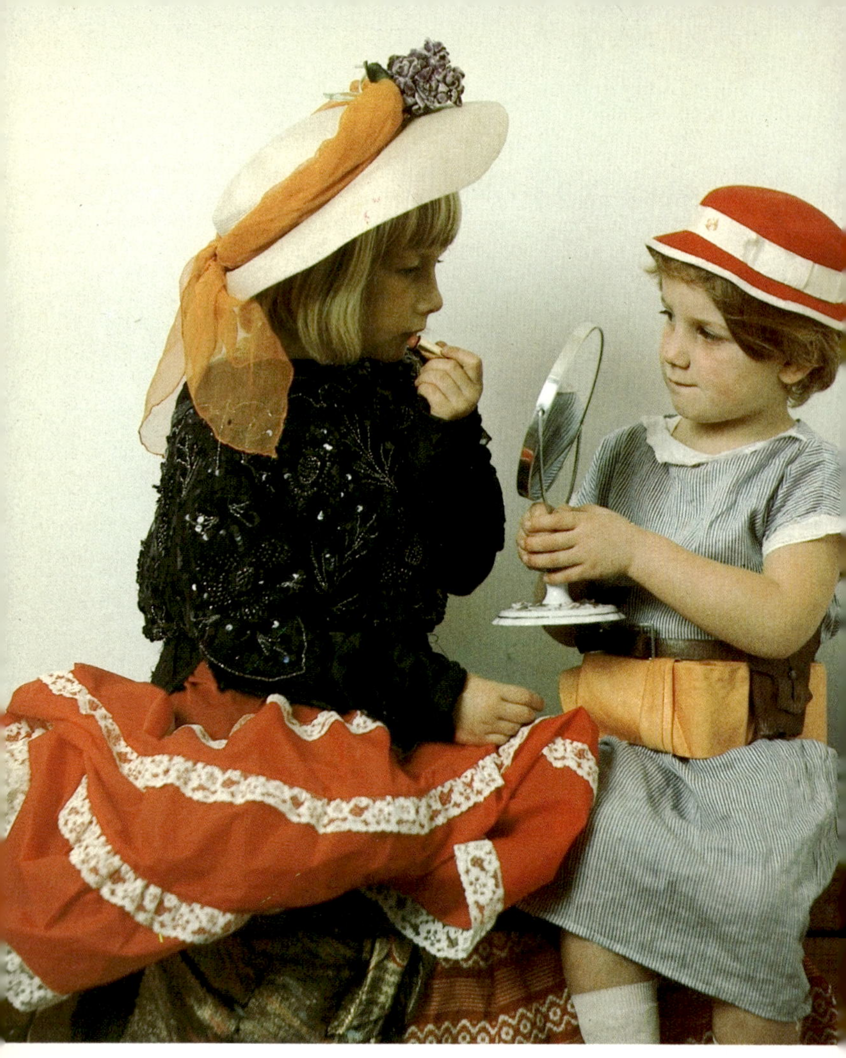

Activities add greatly to pictures of people, especially of children. Simply-arranged lighting, such as bounced flash or paraflash keeps disturbances to a minimum and allows the participants to concentrate on their game – *Alison Trapmore.*

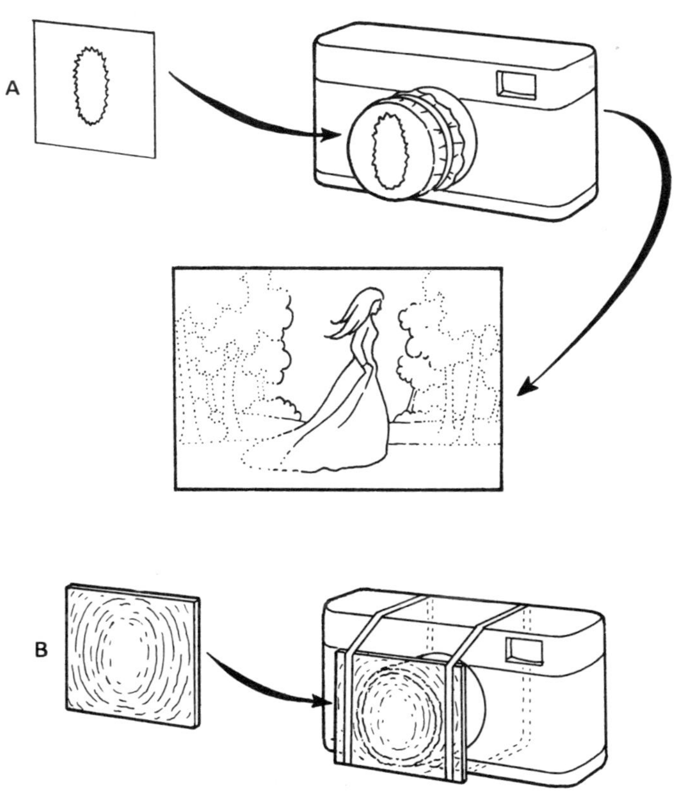


Image softeners. 1. Tracing paper with a hole in the centre attached to the camera with a rubber band. 2. Glass, smeared with petroleum jelly, held in position in front of the lens with two rubber bands.

cover the lens with tracing paper with a hole in the middle so that the person appears in sharp focus when lined up in the centre of the picture. The area surrounding the subject will be blurred by the diffusion of the light through the tracing paper.

The second technique is to smear petroleum jelly onto a small piece of glass which is a bit larger in size than the area of the camera lens. You will want a clear patch in the centre of the glass which has no trace of the jelly on it. Fix the glass onto the camera as shown in the diagram. The amount of diffusion from the jelly depends on how thickly it is coated onto the glass.

Both these techniques obscure the detail surrounding the subject and direct attention to the centre of interest – the person you are photographing. You can obviously use tracing paper or petroleum

BRIDAL PORTRAIT TECHNIQUES

| Emphasis on | | Technique |
|---|---|---|
| A slim line | 1. | Take a side-on view. |
| | 2. | Have her standing rather than seated, a seated curled-up position only really flatters slender girls |
| | 3. | Ask her to take a deep breath before you shoot, this has the effect of improving both line and posture. |
| | 4. | Compose the picture with a vertical format in mind. |
| The legs | | High-heeled shoes or boots have a more slimming effect on the legs than flat shoes or sandals. |
| The eyes | 1. | Focus the camera on the eyes. |
| | 2. | The careful use of make-up helps to make the eyes look larger and more appealing. |
| | 3. | Take head-and-shoulder close-ups. |

jelly with an adjustable camera to achieve equally effective results.
Apart from camera techniques, the other way of creating a flattering image of your girl-friend in particular is to emphasise her attractive features and to play down any prominent ones she may have. This latter topic is covered fully in the chapter on Wedding Photography.
There are several ways of emphasising a girl's best features, these are shown on the table on page 90.
Additional tips on the glamorous aspects of things are given on page 128.
Many of these techniques are equally applicable to photographs of your boy-friend. Naturally you tend to pick out different characteristics in a male portrait. Slimness is not so important, but do avoid emphasis on bad points. A side view, for example, may show up a paunch, or a close view exaggerate a long nose and chin.

# Photographing People Out-and-About

So far we have concentrated mainly on family pictures, particularly of babies and young children, because these are the kind of pictures that most mums and dads want to take. However, as the children grow up their development slows down dramtically, they go through awkward, sometimes spotty, phases, become restless and camera shy and far more interested in their own teenage world than in your hobby of photography. It is at this stage that you may decide to expand your photographic interests in other directions. There are various ways you can do this.

Lots of photographers find a new stimulus through joining a local camera club where they are able to share their experiences with people who have similar interests. Most camera clubs and photographic societies offer a seasonal programme of lectures and discussions covering a wide range of topics. In some clubs there is a strong emphasis on human interest pictures. Others are renowned for the excellence of their pictorial and landscape photography. Some have their own darkrooms where you can learn the art of developing, printing and enlarging your own pictures, usually under the guidance of more experienced members. Once you have been to a few meetings and got into the swing of things, a camera club will certainly help to further your photographic skills.

Another outlet for your talents would be to specialise in portrait photography which you would enjoy if you like the more formal approach to things such as arranging lighting and posing models. If you are interested in branching out in this direction you should read the *Focalguide to Portraits* which contains lots of helpful information on the subject.

On the other hand, you may decide to expand your hobby in the direction of pictures with a general human interest. To do this you need to go out-and-about with your camera, involving yourself in the sort of situations where you will meet people and see things happening. To begin with you will probably have more fun if you limit your horizons to a single activity, perhaps to following a sport with which you or a member of your family has connections; to attending local events, or to supporting your child's scouting activities. Whatever activity you choose to follow and to photograph you will find that once you become an accepted supporter your photographic pursuits will be considered part of the scene. People will become interested in your pictures and, since one thing generally leads to another, you will probably carve a niche for yourself as photographer-in-chief.

As you discover more about the people and the ins and outs of your new interest, you will probably begin to concentrate less on your camera and more on the people you are photographing. Your pictures will certainly become more life-like as you look at people and their activities with a knowledgeable eye rather than as an outsider. You will be able to anticipate expressions and actions when you know what is hapening and position yourself correctly to capture the best view at just the right moment. Being able to appreciate just such subtleties is a great help when you are following a sporting activity.

## Photographing sporting activities

There are several ways you can photograph sportsmen in action to heighten the effects of effort and speed. The method you choose depends on the sport involved as well as on the versatility of your camera.

| Effect | Setting |
|---|---|
| Action frozen, picture completely sharp | Fast shutter speed and small lens aperture |
| A blurred image against a sharp background | Slow shutter speed – action near camera |
| A sharp image against a "moving" background | Panning slow shutter speed with moving camera |
| A partially sharp image against a sharp background | Medium shutter speed and small lens aperature |

Blur effect is often achieved accidentally when parts of the sportsman's body such as the legs of a sprinter or the arms of a javelin thrower, are moving faster than the action-stopping speed of the camera shutter.

## Photographing movement with a simple camera

If your camera shutter functions at a languid pace, you can still get satisfactory results provided you adjust your photographic technique to cater for the limitations of your equipment.

A very effective solution with continuous action sports such as motor racing, cycling or running, is to emphasise the speed of the action rather than to freeze it. To do this, you want to record the subject as a fairly sharp image against a blurred and streaky background. This will happen if you follow or "pan" the subject as the action takes place, keeping the figure in the centre of the viewfinder all the time. As you move the camera, press the shutter release and continue to following the motion without interrupting the smooth panning action. The degree of background blur depends on the speed of the panning. Naturally, that is greatest with fast-moving subjects.

Beware though, if you magnify the image – either through a long-focus (tele) lens, or by subsequent enlargement, you will enlarge the blur just as much. For example, with the 2x tele lens fitted to some pocket cameras, you'll have as much blur from 3m (10 feet) away as you get from 1½m (5 feet) when you photograph with the normal lens.

If you have a practical knowledge of the sport you are photographing you may be able to snap a picture when the action is at a peak. Then the movement halts for a fraction of a second before it starts again in the opposite direction. The pole vaulter at the top of the bar, or a horse rider at the highest point of a jump are examples of such moments when the effects of an action are at a climax. These moments usually coincide with the sportsman adopting his most graceful stance which is another reason why this is a good time to take pictures. During this brief interlude, the relatively slow shutter speed of the simplest cameras can cope quite adequately with the situation.

To create successful pictures, your timing needs to be perfect. The usual cause of disappointing results is that the picture has been taken too late. The secret is to fire the shutter a fraction before the action reaches its peak. This allows just enough time for your reflexes to get to work so that the opening of the camera shutter coincides with the moment of suspended action. If you wait until you see the action reach its peak (when, for example, the diver has reached the top of his spring) then the static moment will be past by the time the camera shutter is ready to record it. The moving figure will photograph as a blurred image if the camera has a relatively slow shutter speed. Even if you can use a high speed and freeze the action, you are likely to get an out-of-balance picture; or even lose part of your subject outside the frame. Once you have taken a few pictures you will soon get the hang of things and discover how to judge the timing to perfection.

Another effective way of recording sporting activities on a simple camera is to shoot from a position where the effects of movement are at a minimum. This occurs when the action is coming straight towards you or going directly away from you. In addition, the effects of movement are less apparent the further they are from the camera. So, if you are photographing a sedate sport you should be able to take sharp pictures of happenings as close as 3m (10 feet) from the camera provided the direction is favourable. However, if the movement is energetic, you will need to consider the camera-to-subject distance as well as the direction of the movement. You should be able to record a sharp image of sportsmen competing 7.5m (about 25 feet) from the camera.

A simple yet effective way of implying motion is by carefully positioning the subject within the picture area. By placing the moving figure along the picture diagonal, so that the subject is tilted in the picture, the impression of motion is much greater than it would be if the figure were upright. Certain actions are obviously more suited to tilting than others but frequently the background determines whether or not tilting the camera will give a successful picture. If nearby trees and buildings are going to feature in the photograph it is almost certain that the tilted view will prove unsatisfactory and look more like a photographer's error than an intentional creative impression.

## Shutter speeds and movement

If you have a shutter speed of 1/250, or better still 1/500th second, you should be able to freeze the action in a considerable number of sporting activities. But, to make the most of an event and to create exciting pictures of the effort and skills that are the trademark of a good sportsman, you will find that you will get the best results by shooting on high speed films. For most people, that means sticking to black-and-white. If, however, there is a specialist laboratory near you – or you process your own – you can use some colour reversal films at high speeds. The increased sensitivity of these films provides you with a far greater choice of shutter speed and lens aperture set-

SHUTTER SPEEDS FOR FREEZING MOVEMENT

| Subject | Approx. speed MPH | Camera-to-subject distance | Direction in relation to camera: Right angles | 45° | Towards or away from |
|---|---|---|---|---|---|
| Slow walking | 2½ | 4.5m 15ft | 1/250 | 1/125 | 1/60 |
| | | 7.5m 25ft | 1/125 | 1/60 | 1/30 |
| | | 15.0m 50ft | 1/60 | 1/30 | 1/15 |
| Fast walking | 5 | 4.5m 15ft | 1/500 | 1/250 | 1/125 |
| | | 7.5m 25ft | 1/250 | 1/125 | 1/60 |
| | | 15.0m 50ft | 1/125 | 1/60 | 1/30 |
| Slow running | 10 | 4.5m 15ft | 1/1000 | 1/500 | 1/250 |
| | | 7.5m 25ft | 1/500 | 1/250 | 1/125 |
| | | 15.0m 50ft | 1/250 | 1/125 | 1/60 |
| Running sports | 20 | 4.5m 15ft | 1/2000 | 1/1000 | 1/500 |
| (sprinting etc) | | 7.5m 25ft | 1/1000 | 1/500 | 1/250 |
| | | 15.0m 50ft | 1/500 | 1/250 | 1/125 |

Note: If you have a telephoto lens which has a focal length about twice that of your standard camera lens, you will need to use the next faster shutter speed to achieve a similar effect. Conversely, with a wide-angle lens which is about half the normal focal length, you need to use the next slower shutter speed to that given in the table. Shutter speeds in excess of 1/1000th second are rare.

tings when you are photographing summer sports. In winter, particularly on dull muddy afternoons, you will need the speed and exposure flexibility of such materials to muster a reasonable shutter speed in the poor lighting conditions.

The table gives a rough idea of the sort of shutter speeds that will be sufficient to freeze actions taking place in various directions in relation to the camera and at different speeds. You might find it helpful to remind yourself of the relevant figures from time-to-time. A good place to keep notes on this or any other exposure information is on a card taped inside the top of your gadget bag or light meter cover so that it's handy when you are out-and-about with your camera taking pictures.

If you intend to shoot a particular action, try to have the camera ready focused on the point where the action peak will occur. So you are all ready to fire the shutter when the action reaches the most dramatic point. To be able to pre-focus the camera accurately, the sport needs to be repetitive like show jumping or gymnastics. When there is no action rehearsal you can use the technique of zone focusing to relieve you of the chore of focusing the camera as the action happens. See page 181.

When you freeze movement with a fast shutter speed the action that you record needs to have quite a bit of impact if the picture is going to look really convincing. You need to choose your viewpoint with care and expose your picture at exactly the right moment to make a really successful shot. This applies particularly if you are shooting on black-and-white film, since the monochromatic image requires additional vitality if it is going to attract attention, especially when seen alongside colour photographs.

If you are using colour print film and your selection of shutter speeds is limited by the film and the low level of the lighting, it is best to forget all about fast shutter speeds and make a point of creating artistic impressions of the sporting scene. You can either use the panning technique described on page 94 in which case the background will be blurred but the competitors fairly sharp, or create the opposite effect of blurred figures against a sharp background. To do this you simply keep the camera stationary so that the background appears sharp and blur the movement by selecting a shutter speed in the region of 1/15 second. You will need to experiment to achieve the most creative effects. It is advisable to use your camera on a tripod or rest it on a firm support, while you are making such long exposures. Otherwise, you may shake the camera and blur the background unintentionally.

## Look for pictures

It is much easier to take successful pictures of sports that you are involved in. If you know the participants and a bit about the rules of the game, you should be able to find good shooting positions to record different stages of the event. Besides the obvious positions at the start and at the finishing line, for example, you will soon find out where exciting incidents may happen. You can be ready, focused and waiting for good picture taking situations to happen.

When you are photographing a local event which is attended by families, friends and a few keen supporters, you will probably be able to get fairly close to the action. By doing so, you feel the tension and excitement of the competition. With all the ferment of the occasion and either luck or a fast film you should not find it too difficult to capture action-packed pictures.

On the other hand, at most big sporting events like Wimbledon, the Olympic Games or a Formula 1 grand prix, you will find it almost impossible to take intimate shots of the competitors from the public seats unless you are lucky enough to be right at the front of a stand. And, even when you are relatively close to the game, you will probably only be able to fill the viewfinder frame with the action if you have a camera fitted with a long focal length lens so that the image size is increased. If you are a follower of sports on television you may have noticed how press photographers are often stationed perilously near to the action: behind the goal, along the touchline or even in specially constructed stands at some events. Vantage points like these are yours for the afternoon at the school sports or local matches and from them you should have plenty of opportunity for exciting photography. When you are looking for good shooting positions you will need to keep an eye on the sun – you won't want it shining straight into the camera lens.

Professional sports photographers make the most of the picture taking opportunities by never trying to economise on film. They take lots of pictures of entire action sequences on motor-driven cameras capable of recording images at the rate of up to 8 or 9 a second. Do not imagine though, that pressing the button on a motor driven camera will give you the ultimate picture every time. Virtually all the best pictures are taken by accurate selection of the ideal moment of exposure. Even without elaborate equipment, you should still aim to be liberal in your use of film as you will stand a better chance of selecting winning pictures if you have more to choose from.

Professionals, though, don't always get special ringside seats. Some of the published pictures of really big events are taken for ordinary spectator sports.

If you are interested in the choice of equipment that is available for sports photography, there is much more information about the subject in the Focalguide to Action Photography.

Generally, the spectators are every bit as photogenic as the sportsmen. Most people will be far too preoccupied with the competition to worry about you and your camera. There are usually good pictures to be had when the climax occurs and cheers of encouragement bellow forth from the most refined-looking spectators, whilst others watch in breathless silence, bodies tense and fists clenched in excitement.

The spectators are one of the attractions at big sporting events, particularly those which have gained a reputation at society gatherings. Fashions are paraded in style and you can really have a ball with a candid camera. Sporting occasions are often patronised by the famous. So keep a good look out for a chance of photographing them. If it is the famous you really want to record, then you should choose suitable events for the crowd rather than the action.

When crowds of people are gathered together you can usually get some appealing pictures of small children peeping past skirts and trouser legs in the general direction of the excitement. If you bend down to shoot you will record the surroundings just as the child sees them. If you want to make a feature of the smallness of the child in contrast to the adults in the background, then the adults should also appear in sharp focus in the photograph. That will mean shooting with the camera lens stopped down to *f*8 or better still to *f*11.

If you really want to make the most of picture possibilities at any sporting event you should always stay until the end. Making a mad dash for the car half an hour before the close of the competition will doubtless save having to sit in the traffic jams but your premature exit might well lose you the best pictures of the afternoon.

**Photographing local events**

Sporting activities are not the only events that are full of action and excitement. You will have just as many opportunities for photographing interesting people at most large outdoor gatherings where the participants are enthusiasts of one sort or another. Veteran or vintage vehicle meetings, agricultural shows, street festivals, funfairs, markets, and a host of other displays and activities abound everywhere. Keep an eye on your local paper, or public notice boards to be in touch.

When you are planning an outing with photography in mind, it's worth taking a couple of extra rolls of film so that you can make the most of picture taking opportunities. If one is a high speed film so much the better because then your photography won't come to a halt the moment the sun goes in.

Whatever the event you will want to be on the lookout for interesting people and weather-beaten characters, fashionable figures as well as colourfully dressed hippies. If the day is one of hazy sunshine you will have plenty of opportunity for using your camera. Any shadows there are will be just barely discernible and will not hinder your photography. Hazy sunshine creates the ideal shooting conditions for taking outdoor portraits so make the most of the situation by taking a few informal close ups to add variety to your picture record. On the other hand if it is bright and sunny you will need to be on the lookout for pictures of people in shaded situations and in areas where the sun is producing side lighting so that the effects of the strong directional light will not spoil your pictures.

At many local events, good pictures are often to be found behind the scenes where the animals are being groomed for the occasion, or the vehicles spruced up for the parade by their doting owners; where nervous competitors pace out their torments, or the Carnival Queen and her entourage undergo last minute titilations as they mount

their flowery chariot for the parade. It is behind the scenes that you will see wide eyed children fascinated with all that is going on and winning competitors proudly adding the latest rosette to the collection on display.
Don't make the mistake of taking only a single picture of each situation you come across. People are constantly changing their expressions and stance and you may not always be lucky and get a natural effect with the first shot. Once you have taken a picture, your camera will be all set up to capture the scene. So you can easily and very quickly wind on, frame up and shoot again if the person you are photographing seems to become more animated or relaxed after the first shot. It is often a good plan to keep looking at the image through the viewfinder as you wind on so that you can be really quick off the mark to take the second picture. Then, even if your subject is aware of the camera, your swift action will not be anticipated and therefore probably help to capture a spontaneous pose.
When you see people engrossed in a particularly interesting activity, you can usually only make a really descriptive account of the event by taking several pictures from different shooting distances and camera angles. If the action is intricate or complicated a single picture will probably contain insufficient detail to make a clear statement. For example, suppose two people are looking under the bonnet of a veteran car. A low angle shot will show their faces in rapt concentration and a second close up will be needed to do justice to the gleaming engine. Similarly, a front view of the bric-a-brac on a stall at an antique market with the dealer in the background could be accompanied by another side-on close-up of a customer paying for a purchase.
Occasionally you see craftsmen giving demonstrations at local events. To fully document their actions, you may need several pictures. A series of shots forms an interesting and more comprehensive account than a single picture would.
Try using your camera in a photojournalistic way to tell complete stories when you are out and about taking pictures at special gatherings. You will find the approach an interesting change from creating the more usual staccato picture record. This pictorial method of reporting events is frequently featured in the Sunday colour supplements. The subjects are usually more colourful and

emotive than those you will probably come across on the local scene. Even so, the photographic techniques are excellent and you could pick up quite a few ideas by studying the picture sequences in detail.

Another place where you frequently find comprehensive and descriptive picture series is in exhibitions displayed for a purpose. For example, those intended to portray the activities of public utilities such as power or water supply companies; and at police, nursing and the forces recruitment centres.

## Off-beat pictures

When you are taking pictures at exciting and emotive places like pop festivals, the conventional approach to photographing people does not always produce pictures that fully convey the mood of the occasion. There are however several off-beat photographic ploys you can use which in themselves creat unusual pictures that help to heighten the impact of the image. These include:

1 Using a slow shutter speed to blur the action of dancers and other fast movements like fingers strumming guitar strings or feet tapping.

2 Photographing silhouetted figures against the orange sky, if there's a good sunset. Details on how to photograph sunsets are given on page 17.

3 Emphasising the emotional impact of the situation, if you do your own developing and printing, by increasing the graininess of your prints. To do this you can, for example, make a big enlargement from a small area of the negative, use a high speed film, or print on a high contrast paper.

4 Selecting a picture format which emphasises the mood of the scene. For example, if a couple are lying stretched out on the grass enjoying the music, by creating a slim horizontally-shaped picture you will add to the feeling of lazy contemplation; conversely, by fitting upright figures inside a narrow vertical format you will accentuate the impression of strength and dignity. If you frame the picture in the viewfinder with the final cropping in mind

you can easily mask the print or transparency to the required format later.

5 Taking pictures at dusk, if you are shooting on colour film, when spot and flood lights illuminate the performers. The artificial lighting will make the colours in your picture appear more red than usual but the contrast between the shadowy figures and the colourful highlights can be most impressive. Exposures at dusk, even with a meter, are unpredictable as the light level will probably be insufficient to give you an accurate reading. If you give a relatively short exposure, the shadows will remain dark and the colours will stand out, whereas with a longer exposure there will be more detail in the shadows but the brightest colours will tend to be overexposed and therefore a bit pale. The shorter exposure gives a more dramatic and effective result.

## Photographing club teams and groups of people

You may be asked to make a special photograph of a group of people, the school football team for example, the contestants in the annual golf tournament or simply the locals outside the pub. Obviously you will want to have a pretty clear idea of how you are going to tackle the task before arriving to take the pictures.

It is worth enquiring beforehand if there is a standard line up for photography which is part of the team or club tradition. Often such groups want an updated version of that, rather than some imaginately posed pictures. You will obviously need last year's photograph to guide you if there is a traditional way of doing things. As well as the grouping of the team, the place you take the picture in is often fixed. If it is, you well advised to study the lighting there beforehand. Then you can confidently recommend the most suitable time to do the job. The day of the photograph may be sunny or cloudy so it is best to choose a time when you know for certain that, if it is sunny, the group will be side-lit. If you get your timing right your pictures will not be spoilt by the sun shining into the camera lens or straight into the eyes of the people in the group.

Once you have arranged the group according to your picture guide you will want to make sure that everyone is looking in the same direction when you press the shutter. That hackneyed expression "say cheese" sometimes works. Better, a well-timed joke usually does the trick and paves the way for a couple of extra pictures. Those extra shots are always worth taking because it is easier to select one really good photograph if you have several to choose from.

If you are able to create your own natural groupings you will want people to appear at different heights in the picture rather than strung out in a line. The easiest way to arrange this is to find some steps or even a robust park bench so that people can cluster around at different levels.

Quite a pleasing arrangement with six or seven people is to form a triangular pattern with two or three people sitting on the ground, two people behind, perhaps sitting on the bench and one person standing at the back to add height to the picture.

Another approach is to find a physical prop for people to gather round, so that there is a natural centre for the grouping. Such a prop could be the goal post or a table with a sun umbrella above, an open sports car or the umpire's chair. You will find that once there is something handy for people to lean on they nearly always settle down and become more relaxed. That is a great help for the photographer. You may need to reposition one or two people to add height to the grouping.

The more light hearted and humourous you make the occasion the better will be your pictures but, however relaxed the atmosphere, the sure way of creating unflattering and awkwardly posed pictures is to keep people hanging about for too long.

## Amateur dramatics

Amateur dramtic societies all want photographs. Approach, or join one, and you will have plenty of opportunity to photograph different aspects of stage life. Your pictures will be in great demand for the society will be only too pleased to have records of their productions. Individual members will want personal copies for their portfolios; and the local press will probably be delighted to publish your pic-

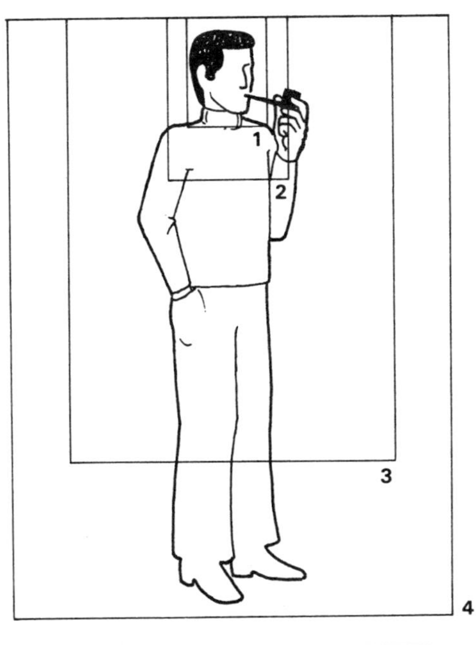


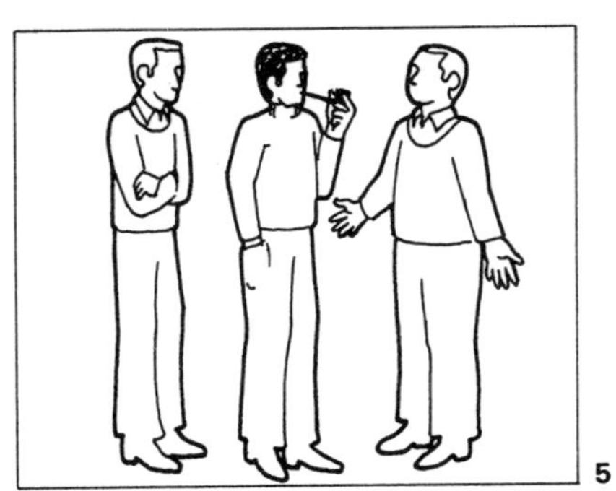


Pictures of people are usually categorised according to the amount of the subject that is included in the negative area i.e. 1. Full head. 2. Head and shoulders. 3. Three-quarter length. 4. Full length. 5. Group.

tures, although they tend to prefer prints that show the entire cast rather than those showing individual performers.
You should have no difficulty photographing actors, either on or off stage, because they are generally the sort of outward-going characters who will act just as well in front of your camera as they will in front of a live audience. Do not forget to picture the sets and costumes as well, though.

## Lighting and film

Your pictures will be more interesting and dramatic if you are able to shoot by available light rather than by flash. To do this you need to have a camera with a lens that has a maximum aperture in the region of *f*1.4. Even with such a fast lens you will need to use a really high-speed film to record natural actions and expressions in the relatively low lighting levels that you will come across in many small theatres and community halls.
When you are exposing colour films to theatre lighting your pictures will not necessarily be of the correct colour balance. Colour inaccuracies, which tend to appear more pronounced in facial close ups than in scene-setting shots featuring several actors, are generally acceptable when the lighting is dramatically coloured.
Colour balance defects tend to be less pronounced in pictures taken on colour negative films as the printing process automatically attempts to normalise colours. In doing so, however, the process lessens the effectiveness of pictures taken in dramatically coloured lighting. Pictures taken on colour transparency film, on the other hand, present colours as they actually are provided the type of stage lighting and the colour balance of the film are compatible. When they are incompatible you can use filters over the camera lens to rectify the situation.
To make certain of successful results you really need to experiment with your film and selection of filters. See the *Focalguide to Filters* for more details.
If you are presented with the opportunity it's worth testing the lighting level on the stage in advance of the session to ascertain if available light photography will be possible so that you can stock up

with high speed film for the occasion, you will probably need to use flash to record scenes on the slower colour films.
Colour is particularly suitable for photographing young children giving dancing displays, as the costumes are usually very bright and cheerful and, when many have been made by the kids' mums, your colourful record will be greatly appreciated. It is preferable to shoot on a colour negative film on such an occasion to ensure that the prints will be of a high standard. (Prints from colour slides are unlikely to be as successful.)
When you are recording outdoor performances you do not have the restrictions imposed on you by the low level of indoor lighting.

## Picture taking opportunities

The conventional time for photographing most stage performances is during a dress rehearsal, when you can move around the stage looking for ideal viewpoints. You usually cannot take photographs at the actual performance. If you did, you would have to shoot from the audience or the wings and the picture possibilities from such distances would be very limited.
You will probably enjoy the picture taking session much more if you read through the play you are to photograph and find out a bit more about the production beforehand. Being familiar with the script has the added advantage of enabling you to anticipate suitable shooting positions and camera angles as well as to time your shooting according to the importance of a particular scene in the play.
It is often impractical for you to be on the stage to photograph ballet, particularly when young children are rehearsing their annual show and prancing about in all directions. But in a small theatre you are usually quite close to the stage positioned in a side box or the circle and from such a high vantage point it would not be too difficult for you to shoot a few general pictures of the performers spanning the stage in attractively patterned groupings.
In the summer, outdoor productions are great fun to photograph and during a performance the audience can be almost as entertaining as the actors themselves. Small children fidget about, bored and uncomfortable on the corporation seating. Pensioner's heads sink

slowly chestwards as their slumbers deepen. They are oblivious of the regimented school children dutifully following the performance under teacher's ever watchful eye. However, it is difficult to record such candid scenes without attracting attention and annoyed comments from people nearby. Matters are improved if you have a long focal length lens and manage to time your shooting to coincide with the noise of passing aircraft or the sound of applause.

## The dramatic effects of distortion

One of the easiest ways of creating dramatic pictures is by photographing people in very high contrast lighting such as that found in night clubs or during the tense moments of a theatrical performance when extremes of lighting are used to heighten the drama. However, a different rather gimmicky approach is sometimes used by advertising photographers to hammer home a particular message. The eye-catching, dramatic appeal of the picture is sometimes created by the use of excessive distortion, a hand, a nose or a foot might appear disproportionately large to the rest of the body.

Distorted pictures can be very effective when they appear larger than life on an advertising hoarding with an appropriate caption like "Your country needs you". The odd distorted image can be quite amusing in a family slide show. Beach settings lend themselves to this type of creative photography as people tend to adopt more relaxed attitudes as they sunbathe and play games. It is easy to creep up on a sleeping model and take close-up pictures from odd angles to emphasise a particular part of the body. Although parts of the body will be at different distances from the camera, you will want them all to appear in sharp focus in the photograph. To achieve this you will want to shoot with a small lens aperture (*f*16 or *f*22 for example).

Excessive distortion is created by:

1. The use of a wide-angle lens rather than the standard camera lens
2. Moving in too close to the subject
3. Shooting from an angle that exaggerates the perspective

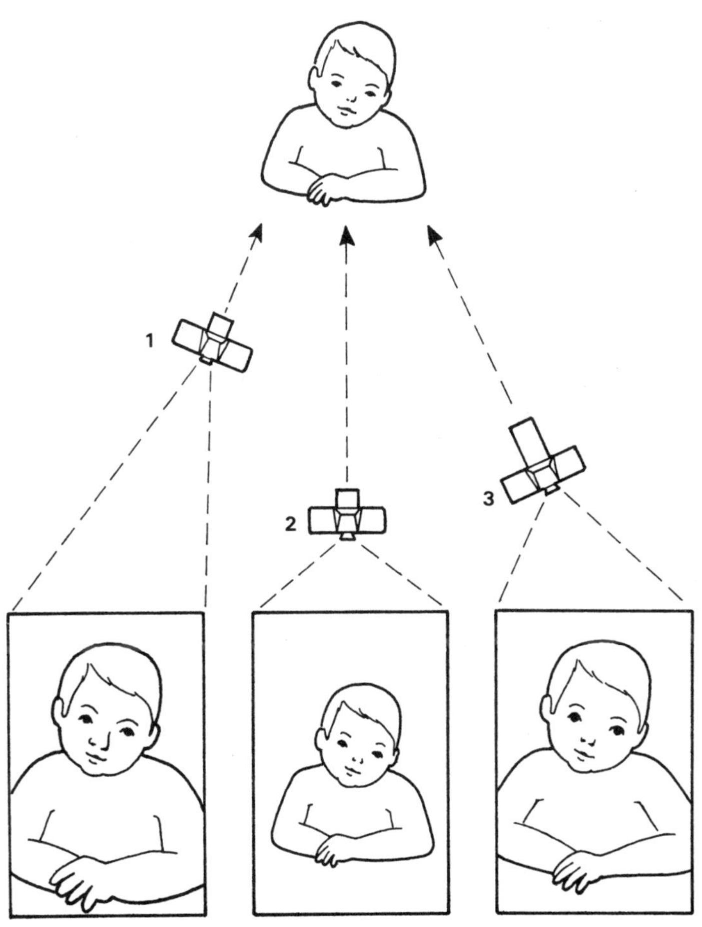


1. Camera too close to subject, resulting picture spoilt by distortion. 2. A shooting distance of about 1.5m gives a distortion-free image but a less intimate view. 3. A long focal-length lens enables you to fill the frame and have an image free from distortion.

Distorted images are generally not as successful when they are confined to a small enprint since the exaggerated perspective of the close view does not have the same degree of impact without the enlargement.

## Photographing silhouettes

Silhouette photographs are fun to take and usually very effective. To be successful, the dark figure must stand out against a brightly-lit background. There are various techniques for creating silhouettes with artificial lighting indoors in a photographic studio. Fortunately, however, similar effects can also be produced outdoors in available light.

The ideal time for creating silhouetted images outdoors is at dusk when background illumination, provided by the setting sun or bright lights, is sufficiently intense to enable the photographer to focus the camera accurately on the foreground figure and shoot with a relatively short exposure. A slightly under-exposed negative or transparency will produce the best silhouette as the under-exposure will ensure that the figure is really black. The background illumination will be extremely striking and for this reason available-light silhouettes are excellent subjects for colour photography.

It's usual to associate silhouettes with figures in profile. Such a side-on view is generally most effective with close shots. When the camera is some distance from the figures in the scene, front or back views can be equally successful.

# Party Pictures

Birthday celebrations, particularly in the form of parties for small children, office parties and dinner dances as well as formal banquets and balls provide a wealth of material for the photographer. There will be numerous opportunities for capturing humorous situations as well as more serious formal moments.

## Childrens' parties

The method of approach depends very much on the age of the children and on the location of the party. Tiny tots at a party are much easier to photograph than their elder brothers and sisters; parties outside are easier to cope with than indoor ones; undoubtedly the easiest event of all to photograph is a party that takes place outside on a warm hazy summer's day. Unfortunately for the photographer, most children's parties seem to take place indoors in rooms that were designed for normal living rather than for a group of children in festive spirit. There is seldom enough space for party games, onlookers or really good photography; but if you pitch in with the idea of catching just a good series of record shots for the family album, you should be well pleased with your results.

There will probably be little opportunity, while the party is in full swing, for mum to pause long enough to think about using the camera at her own children's party. On this occasion photography is usually the métier of fathers and keen helpers.

## Be prepared

Try to use the minimum of photographic equipment so that you can keep a tight hold on it while it is in use, or hide it in an unobtrusive corner if you are required for other things. Have a spare roll of film at the

ready just in case you get trigger happy during the opening stages of the party and run out half way through. If the party is indoors you will need to have plenty of flash in reserve as well.
Most children's parties consist of an eating session and a playing session. Of the two, the eating is often the funnier and more rewarding from the photographic point of view. Fortunately for the photographer the children are usually reasonably still, and usually seated at a table. So, you will have time to frame up and focus on several good-looking pictures without fear of the subject disappearing from view. For a while they are unlikely to bother about you or your camera as they succumb to the lure of sausage rolls, crisps, jellies and birthday cake. This is the time you should be ready with your camera just waiting to make the most of picture-taking situations as they crop up.

## Camera angles

If you want a picture of all the guests enjoying the feast it is best to shoot from a fairly high camera angle. If possible, stand on a chair or a stool so that you are looking down on the table to take the photograph. It's quite a good idea to line this shot up before the party begins. View the table from several different high shooting positions so that when the time comes you will know exactly where to put the stool for the best possible results. The advanced planning will save you having to interrupt the feast at an inopportune moment and spoil the tempo of the occasion. Hungry and excited youngsters will probably not take kindly to an over-enthusiastic photographer rearranging them and the furniture for a photograph.
With a high camera angle you will be able to record, in detail, the table setting with all its colourful dishes and party trappings. In addition, such a shooting position provides greater opportunity than would a normal camera angle to include all the guests in the scene. Take your over-all shots as soon as the meal begins. Quite shortly, the table will look a total shambles and all the plates will be bare.
Whenever you are shooting indoors from a high camera angle, you will be tilting the camera downwards and vertical lines appearing in the outer edges of the scene will converge toward the bottom of the

photograph. The convergence of these lines tends to be accentuated by the dead straight edges of the print or transparency frame. The distraction will be less if vertical lines in the centre of the picture are truly vertical. It is always best to try and arrange a high angle picture so that things such as fireplaces, picture frames and door frames are well to the centre of the scene.

Indoors you may find that the most satisfactory camera position is from a high angle looking into the dining room through the doorway. This is frequently the only possible camera position when lots of children are crowded into a small room for the birthday tea.

When the fun and games begin you will want to shoot from a fairly low angle so that the camera is on the same level as the party guests.

## Family celebrations

Parties and dances are ideal events for photography as people will be too busy enjoying themselves, gossiping with old friends and sampling the good food and drink to worry about the camera. With special parties like silver wedding anniversaries and those to celebrate a teenager's coming of age, you will want to take pictures of the speeches and toasts as well as the cake cutting and shots of the guests enjoying themselves.

When elderly folk are celebrating it is worth making the effort to take a special family group of all their children and the grandchildren together, particularly if the family is scattered and seldom gathers in full strength. If you want to achieve the most pleasing result you will have to:

1. Take the picture in diffused lighting
2. Move in close to take the picture so that the group fills most of the image area
3. Arrange the family artistically so that their heads are not all on the same level
4. Have the older members of the family sitting down with others sitting in front and the men standing behind
5. Catch everyone's attention as you are about to shoot so that they will all be pictured looking toward you

## Office parties

The most usual time to think about work and photography is when there is a celebration or a party in the offing. But, unfortunately, all too frequently when there is no staff photographer to do the honours such thoughts usually happen on the day of the party just when the presentations or the speeches are being made. This is generally far too late to organise films and flash and camera gear so the event passes unrecorded. In fact, it's at just such parties, particularly when a member

SUMMARY OF FILMS AND LIGHTING FOR PARTY PICTURES

| Location | Lighting | Suitable films | Picture possibilities |
|---|---|---|---|
| Indoors | Flash-on-camera* | Colour print film (so that you can easily have copies made for party friends). | Record shots |
| | Available light | High-speed films – colour slide or black-and white | Creative pictures. |
| Outdoors | Available light | Colour print film or any colour slide film** | Record shots and creative pictures. |

*If you have electronic flash and are able to bounce the light from the ceiling as well as operate the camera you may be able to take a couple of soft-lit shots of the party table. Once the serious eating starts there will probably be too much activity for you to indulge in such creations. (For details on bounced flash see pages 183–188.)
**If the party is taking place in a large garden children will probably rush around and get very excited. To capture sharp images of moving subjects you will need to shoot on high-speed film.

of the staff is retiring or leaving the company, that a camera really comes into its own for creating a pictorial account of the event as well as a lasting souvenir of familiar friendly faces, the tributes and the merrymaking.

## Picture possibilities

When a member of staff is retiring or leaving the company you will want to include everybody that's at the party in at least one of your pictures. This is not a difficult task because the principal guest usually makes a point of chatting to everyone present. If you wait until three or four people are in conversation and photograph mainly groups you should soon have a good collection of pictures of the complete assembly.

You should be able to snap a few unposed shots but, if space is limited, you may well have to ask people to move around a bit so that you can get a better view. You will find your pictures much easier to compose if the people in them are standing rather than sitting down. In the sitting position you have the untidy complication of people's legs, tables, chair legs and handbags cluttering up the bottom half of the photograph.

The presentations and speeches usually assume a slightly formal tone so you will want to be prepared to photograph the ceremony with sufficient film in your camera to record:

1. The boss giving his speech
2. The handing over of the gift
3. The thank-you speech
4. Cutting the cake (if there is one)

When you are sorting through the pictures to show to your colleagues, you will want to number the prints so that they are easily identifiable. Then, if you wait to send for the reprints until everyone has had a chance to ask for copies, you will be able to place one large order and possibly benefit from a reduction in price as a result of the quantity printing.

If you are taking photographs at a conventional office party, you will want to picture your friends having fun, gossiping and dancing together and enjoying the food and drink.

## Formal occasions

Photography is often easier at formal occasions such as banquets and celebration dinner dances than it is at less formal gatherings. That's because there is usually a set programme of toasts and speeches through which the photographer will be guided by the Master of Ceremonies. Speeches are generally made by the guests on the main table which makes the task of picture taking a relatively simple one as most shots can be taken from a single camera position.

## Camera angles and lighting

Occasionally, at some really formal dinners, the principal guests are seated at a higher table than everyone else. When this happens you will want to take pictures from a similar elevation. A low shooting angle, which tends to be unflattering particularly with elderly people, is even more detrimental in the harsh lighting of direct flash.

## Lighting indoors

The most practical general lighting for indoor photography at parties or on more formal occasions is flash-on-camera. It enables you to take pictures easily and wander freely among the guests looking for good photographic possibilities. Generally parties are not the time to go in for the more subtle forms of lighting. They need extension cables and other delicate photographic paraphernalia which will be very vulnerable to damage by the party guests. At some daytime parties, particularly those in large, well-lit modern offices it may be possible to shoot by available light.

Flash-on-camera is a rather harsh form of lighting. However, there are several ways you can minimise the derogatory effects of the direct illumination. The most obvious is to take full advantage of the flexibility of movement that it affords by choosing imaginative camera angles for some of your pictures. In addition to the suggestions given in the Flash facts table on page 183 the following points are particularly relevant party to situations:

When you are taking pictures through a doorway, make sure that the flash is actually pointing into the room and not straight at the door-frame or an adjacent wall. If the flash fails to light the scene in the room the resulting photographs will be under-exposed and the party guests will picture as dark shadowy figures against an even darker background. "Computer" electronic flash is particularly prone to this problem. The sensor cuts off the flash as soon as enough light is reflected from the subject. If you let even a little of the flash spill onto a close-by wall, you will reduce the light falling on your main subject.
Large glass windows, which are a feature of so many modern offices, reflect light like any other shiny surface such as oak panelling, wine glasses, silver tankards and trophies and even people wearing spectacles. Such surfaces are all capable of reflecting the light straight back into the camera lens if the camera and the flash are pointing directly at them. To avoid spoiling your pictures by unnecessary blotches of reflected light, try to make a point of framing up on shots from such a position that the camera and the flash are at a slight angle to the offending surface. Then, in all probability, any reflected flash light will be reflected away from the camera.
Formal dinners usually take place in large halls where the tables are arranged well away from the room walls. This is ideal for flash-on-camera photography because it means that your pictures should be free from the harsh shadows which so often spoil flash-on-camera shots of groups of people in small rooms.
Avoid including people in your pictures who are sitting or standing at different distances from the camera. The fall-off in light from the flash increases dramatically at increased distances, so someone who is twice as far from the flash as the principal subject for whom the flash exposure was calculated, will only receive one quarter of the exposure and therefore be hard to recognise in the shadowy depths of your photograph.

## Lighting outdoors

At most outdoor parties the table is set in a shady spot which is ideal for the photographer. The soft lighting in the shade is perfect for recording close faces and expressions – these will abound as the food is enjoyed and the party begins to swing.

When the subjects are in the shade, it is best to take pictures with the camera looking into the shade; rather than out towards the sunshine. This positioning is important if your camera has a built-in light meter. The meter will give a reading for the average brightness of the scene. This reading will be high if the sunny background is included in the scene and the children in the shade will be under-exposed in the resulting photograph.

When you are taking pictures outdoors in various lighting conditions, and you are using a camera that is not automatic, you will need to remember to adjust the exposure to suit the different levels of lighting in open shade, full sun, side light, etc., in order to get consistently well-exposed pictures.

## Choice of film

A colour print film must be the first choice for recording party pictures as quite a few people will want to have copies of your photographs. If you are taking pictures at a formal gathering or an office presentation you may be asked to submit prints to the local newspaper or staff magazine. Black-and-white enlargements, rather than colour prints, are generally required for reproduction.

It is possible to have black-and-white prints made from colour negatives but, before you decide to shoot in colour and have the odd monochromatic enlargement made from the appropriate colour negatives, it is worth phoning the photographic establishments in your area to make sure that someone is in a position to provide such a service.

Making your own top quality, black-and-white prints from colour negatives calls for working in total darkness because to get first class results you need to use special printing paper that is fully colour sensitive (panchromatic). The usual monochrome printing paper (such as bromide) is not colour sensitive. It does not give accurately toned prints from colour negatives. When you are using bromide paper you can, of course, work in subdued safelighting which greatly simplifies matters.

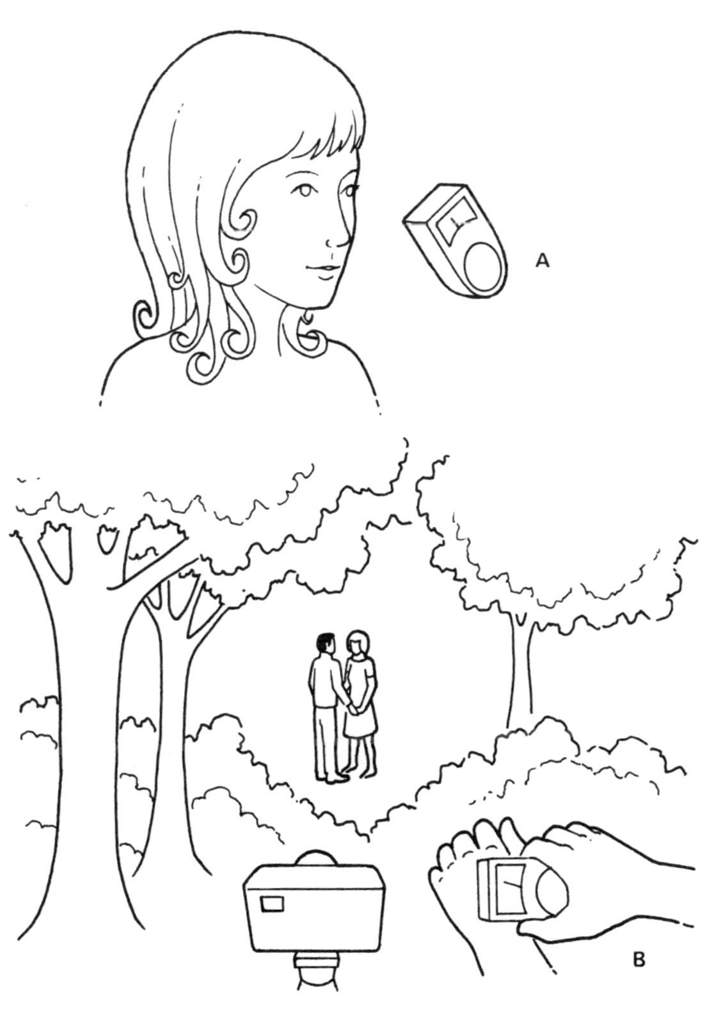


Using an exposure meter. To make an accurate exposure assessment you can either take a reading close to the subject (A) or substitute the back of your hand for the subject and take a reading from that. (B).

## Special equipment

Although you can get satisfactory results photographing parties on any camera, if you intend to enlarge your negatives to provide prints of a suitable size for reproduction, you will be wanting the additional picture sharpness afforded by the better quality lenses of a more sophisticated, adjustable camera.

A great asset when you are shooting under cramped conditions is a camera fitted with a wide-angle lens. The additional covering power of short focal length lenses enables you to record a far greater subject area than you could with a standard camera lens.

# Photographing Weddings

When your friends know about your photographic talents it won't be that long before you get an opportunity to prove your abilities at a wedding. At first you might be asked to take some extra pictures, a few informal shots of the guests arriving at the church and enjoying the reception. As one thing usually leads to another, you may eventually be requested to completely cover a wedding ceremony.

However willing you are to accept such responsibilities, you are not being fair to yourself or to your friends if you are only used to using a simple camera. Wedding photography requires a camera that is equipped with controls for both shutter speed and lens aperture. That is because weddings happen without regard to good photographic conditions and, having committed yourself to taking photographs, you need to be able to cope with the task whatever the weather.

Another important aspect to consider is that the sequence of events that you can anticipate at a wedding depends upon the religious following of the families involved. The ensuing details relate to Anglican Christian weddings. However, the photographic requirements of the bride and groom may not follow the same pattern if the religious service is conducted differently. If you do happen to be asked to take photographs at a wedding for friends whose religion is different from your own, you will want to find out what will be expected of you well before the day.

## Informal wedding pictures

If you have established that you are taking fill-in pictures and not the formal photographs you can sit back and relax. Apart from your usual camera gear you will need an extra roll or two of film and to be able to cater for a few more flash pictures than usual. A quick trip to the local supplier, then you should be all ready for the day.

## Which film?

The sort of pictures you will be taking, people enjoying a special occasion, will get shown around. The wedding couple will want to see them, the parents will want to show them to their particular side of the family, the bride will want to show them to her friends – they will certainly go on tour. So you need to use a print film rather than one that gives transparencies. And, of course, you will want to shoot in colour to do justice to the occasion.

Colour transparency films are not really suitable for wedding photography when extra pictures are certainly going to be required. Slides are more cumbersome to show around than colour prints and need to be seen projected in a darkened room to be really effective. Although it is possible to have colour prints made from colour slides the results are often disappointing. Picture contrast increases on reproduction. A wedding, with all its black-and-white clothing, is a high contrast subject and a print made from a high contrast transparency is extra harsh and lacking in detail. If you stick to a colour negative film you'll be far more satisfied with the results and any additional prints you have made will be just as good as the original ones.

## What sort of lighting?

The outdoor pictures you will be taking will require the same sort of exposure treatment as any other outdoor pictures of people. If it is sunny you will want to avoid taking pictures when people are looking into the sun and make full use of any open shade you can discover.

For pictures at an indoor reception you will need to use flash. Before the event make sure that you have enough flashes to take a couple of films. There is nothing worse than running short just as things start to become less formal and the guests get to know each other.

You can now get fast (400 ASA) print films. These allow you to take pictures without flash in brightly-lit churches or receptions . However, they are decidedly granier than normal (100 ASA) films. So, use them only when you need them.

## Picture taking ideas

As the bride or groom will probably be a family friend, you will be able to chat about possible pictures before the wedding day. The couple may already have an idea of the range of shots the professional photographer will take. There's no point in duplicating these pictures.

When you are talking to them, stress that you will be taking mainly off-beat, informal shots to convey the feeling of the event. A wedding is an emotional occasion, there will be solemn moments as well as a little sadness, but many happy times too. These are the sort of situations that create great opportunities for candid pictures.

The following list of picture possibilities may give the bride a few ideas and, having read it, she will probably make suggestions and request additional pictures. Write down her comments so that you'll have a descriptive photo shopping list to mull over before the day.

"Fill-in" picture suggestions:

. the bride at home having a dress rehearsal with the bridesmaids
. the couple at the altar*
. special family friends
. elderly relations
. disabled guests
. young friends and relations
. the wedding presents on display

If you are asked to take photographs at the bride's home before the wedding day there are several situations that make good pictures. Have a look round before you start shooting and discover possible settings for your pictures. Perhaps there is a mirror in one of the bedrooms which would make an attractive setting for a shot of the bride arranging her veil, or a well lit French window which might be used as a frame to a full length picture. Alternatively, the garden might be a good setting for photography, particularly if it contains attractive flowers and trees.

If you intend to concentrate your efforts on a few head-and-shoulder portraits you should aim to take the sort of pictures that the bride

*Photography is not allowed in some churches so you will need to check beforehand.

herself is going to like. That means taking pictures that are well-lit and carefully posed to give an attractive profile.

### Let's consider the lighting first

Without a doubt you will get the most pleasing results by taking the pictures outside in the garden in diffused lighting. The soft even lighting on an overcast or hazy day will enable you to capture all the intricate detail of the dress and veil and will emphasise the softness and colour in the bride's face.

You will get a similar effect by shooting in a shaded part of the garden on a sunny day. The ideal spot is where the background is fairly uniform in colour so that the whole emphasis of the picture is focused on the bride.

Sometimes, you just can't get away from the sun. In that case, you need fill-in flash to give you reasonably well-lit pictures (see p. 192). Be careful, though, that you use the flash just as a fill. Fully flash-lit outdoor wedding pictures really look artificial.

If you have to take the pictures indoors you can either arrange the bride near a well lit window and shoot by available light (see page 24) or, alternatively, you could use one of the flash techniques described on page 182).

When you have selected a suitably lit location for the pictures you will need to give the bride a few directions before you start shooting. Although she might be a little nervous she will want to do all she can to help you to make a good job of the photographs.

She will feel much more relaxed if she can do something other than stand and look at the camera. Give her an attractive flower to hold or find something that she can lean her arms on so that she is not all stiff and tense.

While you are chatting about this and that, study the scene in the camera viewfinder from all possible angles, and a few different camera to subject distances. Ask her to keep her body still and to simply follow your movements with her head and eyes. You are bound to find that some camera positions give much more pleasing pictures than others. The annotated diagram on page 129 will help you to find the most flattering position for a portrait picture.

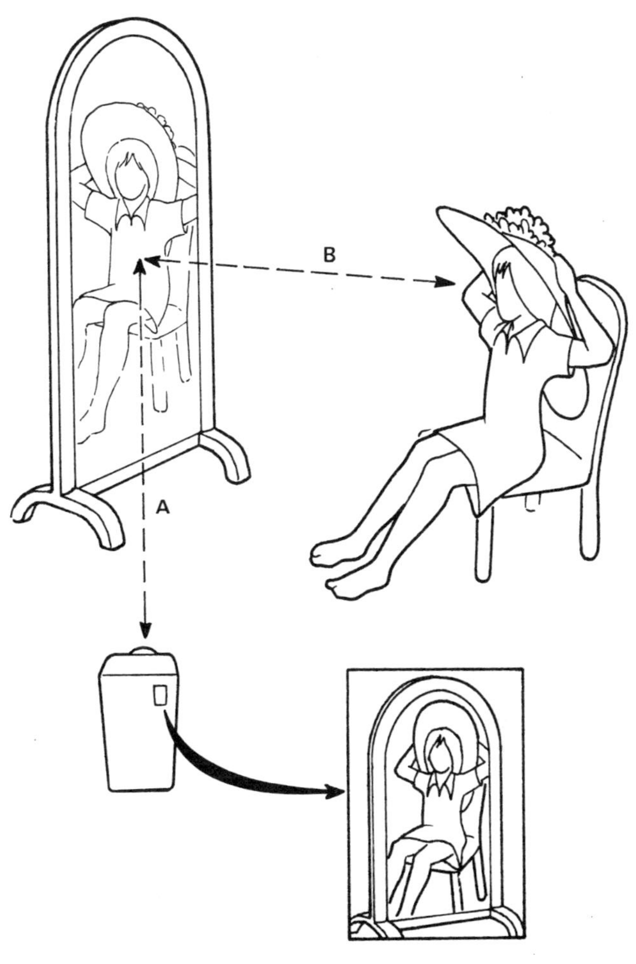


Mirror images. If your camera has a subject-distance setting, the focusing distance for a mirror shot is A plus B (the sum of the distances from the camera to the mirror and the mirror to the subject).

## Corrective treatment for problem faces

If the bride has any obvious prominent facial features you can minimise these in the photographs by careful choice of camera angle. For a head-and-shoulder portrait it is usual to have the camera on a level with the subject's eyes. Raising the camera slightly so that you are looking down onto the subject has the effect of narrowing and lengthening features. Conversely, lowering the camera so that you are looking slightly upwards at the subject flattens and broadens facial features.

| Use a low camera angle to reduce the effects of a . . . | Use a high camera angle to reduce the effects of a . . . |
|---|---|
| Long nose | Short nose |
| Short neck | Long neck |
| Narrow chin | Prominent jaw |
| Prominent forehead | Narrow forehead |

## Full length shots

When you are taking full length shots of the bride alone, or surrounded by the bridesmaids, you will need to arrange the train of the dress artistically to get a pleasing picture. The most flattering photographic angle is to have the bride in semi profile. This emphasises the line of her dress and the slimness of her figure. If she is at a loss as to what to do with her hands and arms a neat solution is for her to clasp her hands gently together below her waist. Group the bridesmaids around the bride so that they are clustered around her rather than strung out in a line. If there are several bridesmaids and pageboys as well, have the smaller children stand in front of the taller ones.

## On the wedding day

On the day of the wedding make sure that you don't impede the professional photographer. You will probably use your camera most after the ceremony while the official pictures are being organised.

Keep on the look out for humorous happenings as the youngsters rediscover their legs and lungs. While people chat and watch the bride and groom, try to take a few close-ups of heads and hats and the elderly relations as well as the shots the bride has requested.
Be ready when the bride and groom depart for the reception and the confetti rains down on them. And, if you have any film left after the reception, try to get a final shot of the guests waving farewell to the couple as they depart for their honeymoon, or a shot of the car as they drive away.

**Formal wedding pictures**

If the only wedding pictures you have ever been involved in were your own, you probably won't remember all that much about how the photographer organised things. Now that you are going to be on the other side of the camera, in command, you will need to find out the general routine before the big day. Have a look through your own or a friend's wedding album to see if you can pick up any ideas from the pictures. Go along to the local church and watch the photographer in action. See how he organises different groupings around the wedding couple, how he cajoles the guests into order and catches their attention just at the right moment as the shutter fires. You cannot help but be impressed by the performance of a good wedding photographer.
If you begin to have second thoughts about taking pictures remember it will be much easier for you to organise people whom you know. You will be able to ask Mr Smith to stand by Mrs Smith and to tell Aunt Jane to move in closer. There will be none of "would the lady in the white hat, yes you madam, face the camera – thank you" which can make the going rather hard.

**Be prepared**

Make a point of inspecting the scene a few days before the wedding and at about the same time as the ceremony. See the direction of the light and find the best areas for photography. Select spots with

regard to the background. Attractive porches or plain walls feature most frequently in wedding pictures as they provide a relatively neat background for the complicated group pictures.
Take an exposure meter with you (unless your camera has a built-in meter) and take a few readings so that you can plan what camera exposures you will want to use for the different shots. Remember to cater for both bright sun and cloudy conditions.

## The final check

1. Have you enough film? (You will probably take about 40 pictures)
2. Is your camera working properly?
3. Have you enough flash? (See that any batteries are fully charged)
4. Are you sure of the route from the church to the reception?

Don't leave this check until the last minute just in case you have to call in outside help.
Have a standby supply of fast black-and-white film for taking out-door pictures if the weather is really bad.

## Use a tripod

Many wedding photographers like to put the camera on a tripod, particularly when they are taking the group pictures. Apart from looking impressive, a tripod creates a focal point for the guests to cluster round. It also leaves the photographer free to move about and to organise things while the picture remains set up in the viewfinder.
Heavy, steady tripods are just the thing for wedding photography. Another asset if you do have a tripod is a cable release. This is a gadget that enables you to fire the shutter without touching the camera so that once the picture is correctly framed in the viewfinder and is in sharp focus you can concentrate on the subject rather than on the camera.

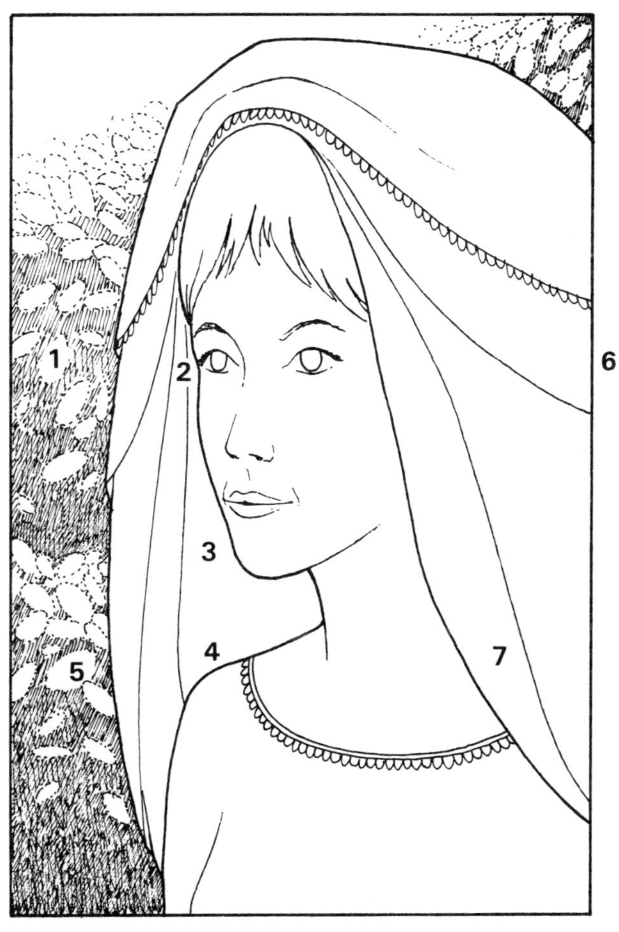


Features of a bridal portrait. 1. Picture balance created by leaving space for the eyes to look into. 2. Camera focused on the eyes. 3. Head in semi-profile. 4. Sholders at an angle to the camera. 5. Background out-of-focus. 6. 35mm format – camera held vertically. 7. Veil attractively arranged.

## Pictures at the church before the ceremony

1. Groom, best man and ushers.
If they arrive together you may get a chance to take a group picture.
2. The guests.
If you photograph them while they are walking towards the church you will need to use a shutter speed of 1/250 second to freeze the movement. At a country church there may be an attractive entrance gate which would make an ideal frame for these shots.
3. The bridesmaids.
Group them together with the smaller youngsters at the front. The attractive dresses and colourful bouquets will create a very pleasing picture.
4. The bride and her father.
Try to get a full length shot as they enter the church. The bride is likely to have her veil covering her face – do not ask her to raise it.

## During the ceremony

When the guests are inside the church you will want to get out your flash gear ready for the next shot and to change the film in your camera before you enter the church if there are only a few shots left. There is nothing more off putting to a photographer than to have to change the film at an inappropriate moment.
If you have a tripod it is a good idea to leave it tucked out of sight in the entrance lobby. You can pick it up on your way out of the church after the ceremony.

## Pictures after the ceremony

1. Signing the register
As soon as the religious ceremony is over the couple will sign the register in the vestry. The parson will probably be quite used to photographers recording this scene and will probably know exactly where you should put the camera. Most vestries are so small that

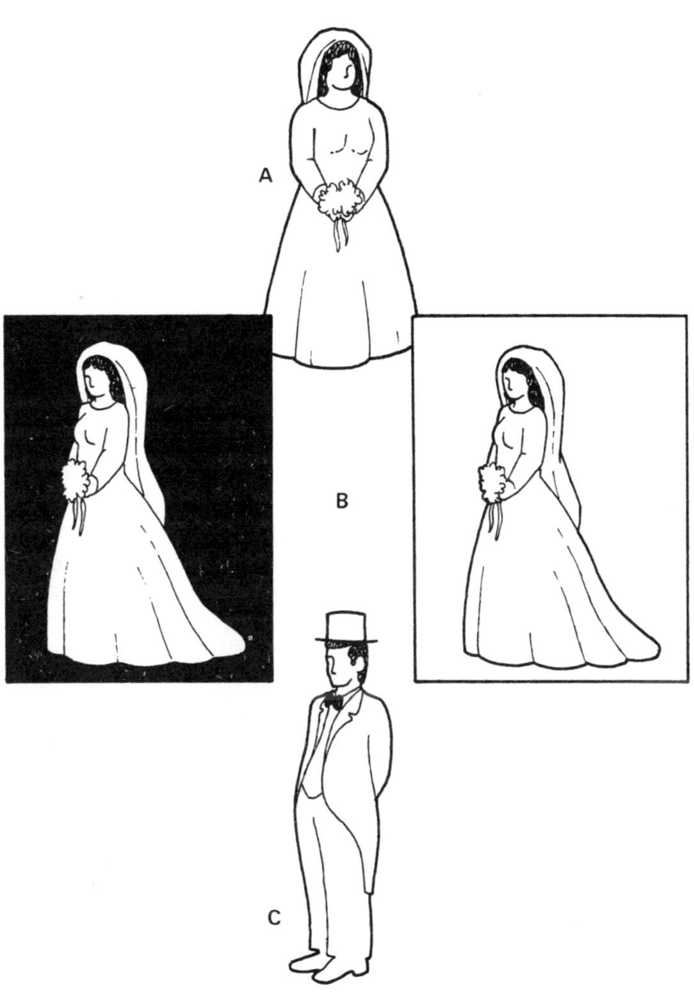


Portly brides. A frontal view has the effect of broadening even the slimmest of figures (A). A side-on view shows off the dress to advange. A dark background emphasises the fuller figure whereas a light one produces a much slimmer effect (B). A portly groom is a different matter! (C).

there is little room for photographic artistry. A straightforward flash-on-camera shot will record the scene.

2. Walking down the aisle

You need to gather up your things faily speedily and make your way to the church entrance so that you are framed up and ready to shoot as the couple walk down the aisle together. The flash-to-subject distance will be greater in this shot than in the previous one so you will need to adjust your lens setting aperture accordingly. (Or make sure you are within the "automatic" flash range.)

3. The group pictures

This is where that tripod will come in handy. Most of the guests will want copies of these pictures so you will want to make quite sure of your focusing. Use a small lens aperture for the large groups to ensure maximum sharpness over the entire picture area (*f*8 or *f*11). Try to capture everyone's attention just as you are ready to shoot. A witty remark can work wonders.

4. Leaving the Church

Once the formalities are over people will be chatting and congratulating the happy couple. Your last shots before the reception should show the couple by the wedding car with perhaps a flash-on-camera shot of them sitting inside it.

5. At the reception

The one formal flash shot you will need to take is that of the bride and groom cutting the wedding cake. The way in which you do this depends very much on the surroundings. Ideally you should show the couple at the side of the cake rather than behind it with both their hands on the knife as it touches the icing.

There will probably be quite a few other cameras recording the informal shots of the couple chatting to their friends and meeting new relations, of the toasts and the speeches and the couple leaving for their honeymoon. So why not put your camera away, relax and enjoy yourself.

## Register-office weddings

The usual time for photography at such an occasion is after the register has been signed and the formalities have been completed.

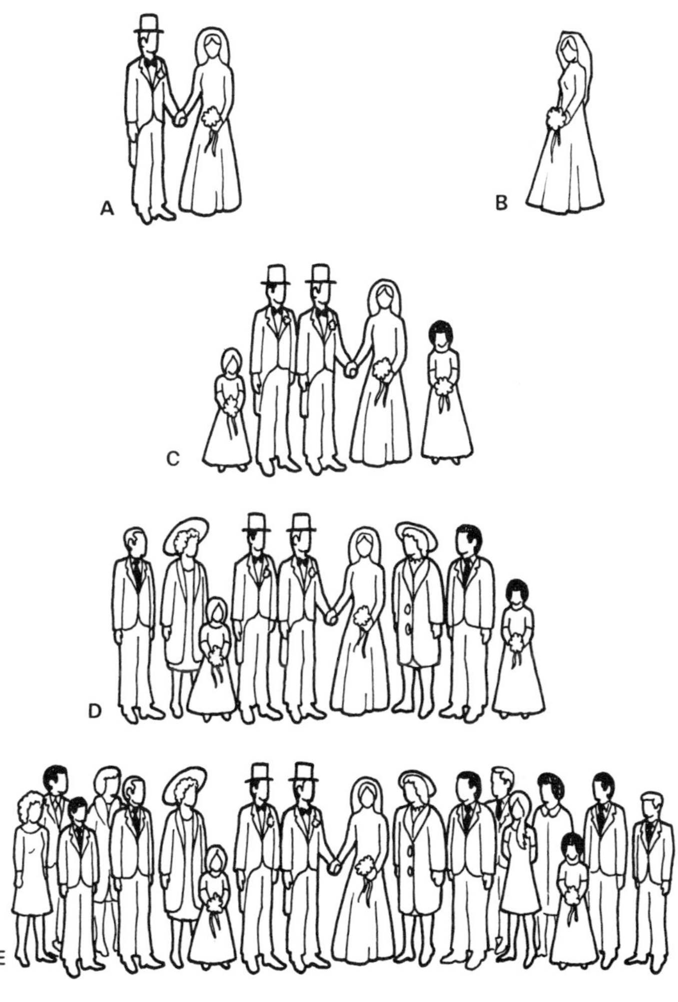


The wedding line-up. A. Groom and bride. B. Bride alone. C. Bridesmaid(s), best man, bride, bridesmaid(s). D. Groom's parents, bridesmaids(s), best man, groom, bride, bride's parents and bridemaid(s), E. The wedding party.

The groupings of parents and guests around the bride and groom are similar to those at a church wedding. If there are a few people at the registry itself, the wedding couple may want you to take lots of pictures of friends and relations gathered at the reception. If this is the case you will probably be requested to take a few formal groupings as well as a record shot of the bride and groom cutting the cake. As you are moving around taking informal shots of the guests, make a point of including everyone present on at least one picture so that the wedding album will be a complete record of the event.

## Presenting your wedding pictures

The final touch, and just as important as the wedding photography, is for you to display your pictures to advantage in an attractive wedding album. It takes time, care and patience to make up a really good album that both you, the wedding couple and their families will be proud of. The time will be taken up making sure that all the pictures sit neatly trimmed and carefully positioned on the pages. Care will be needed to ensure that the white covers and pages of the album remain in an immaculate condition while you work on them.
A good place to start looking for wedding albums is on the advertisement pages of a photographic magazine. You can usually find the addresses of several companies offering descriptive brochures of their different photographic mounts and wedding albums.

# Photographing People on Holiday

Many camera owners take more pictures on holiday than they do at any other time of the year. This is not surprising since there is usually more time to think about photography when you are not having to cope with the rush and bustle of a working week. As you unwind on holiday and start to enjoy yourself, everything begins to look more cheerful and colourful so it is quite natural for you to want to reach for the camera and record the fun.

Part of the enjoyment of a holiday is seeing and meeting different people, making new friends, chatting to guests in the hotel, or swapping stories with the locals over a drink or two. Everything is so fresh and animated that you should have lots of scope for making successful pictures. And, if you holiday abroad, there will be so many new faces and fascinating scenes to photograph that you will have a hard job to contain your enthusiasm.

## Planning before you go

It can be quite interesting, particularly if you are going abroad, to find out in advance a bit about the places you will be visiting on holiday. Have a look for relevant books in the travel section of your local library or bookshop; study the travel agency brochures and any tourist guides that you can acquire before you go away. Some of these publications will undoubtedly be illustrated with maps and photographs. The pictures might give you a few ideas of the sort of conditions you are likely to encounter on holiday. They cannot possibly tell you the whole story, they are simply an appetizer, the rest will be waiting for you on arrival.

Some advanced knowledge is particularly useful if you are about to embark on a touring holiday. There is nothing more annoying than to make a special detour to visit a place that is well known perhaps for its market day, weekly bull fight or monthly auction sales, to find that you are a couple of days early or a day or two late. Such mishaps could easily be avoided with a bit of forward planning which, if you are equipped with the right books and reliable travel guides, can be done at a leisurely pace long before you set off on your travels.

## Holiday films and camera gear

Another aspect of advanced planning concerns films. It is generally more convenient to buy your films before you go on holiday and usually cheaper too if you are going abroad. If you are not particularly photographically orientated, it is wise to take your holiday pictures on films with which you are familiar, rather than to experiment with new ones. You won't want to spend precious time in the photo shop bothering about film speeds and other technicalities when you could be out having fun, or to return home and discover that you had used a new film incorrectly and your holiday pictures were not up to standard.

How much film? It is a difficult question to answer because the amount you need depends on the length of your holiday and on the things you plan to do. If you are a keen sunbather you will probably take less pictures than someone who is out and about exploring places and meeting people. The number of pictures you take also depends on how sharp you are at recognising situations with picture potential. If you are a keen photographer, touring with a camera, you should have enough film to cater for an average of 10 pictures a day (4 x 36 exposure films for a 2-week trip). You can always bring back unexposed films and keep them in a cool place, such as the refrigerator, for another occasion. Of course, if your main purpose is photography, you may want far more film. If that is the case, I am sure you can work out your own needs.

It is a good plan to keep all your photographic gear together while you are away on holiday. Most photographers use a gadget bag for this purpose. Another item which may come in handy and is a useful thing to have with you just in case, is a polythene bag which is large enough to comfortably hold the camera and a spare roll of film. If the beach is very sandy or the holiday weather rather wet, the bag will come in very useful to protect the camera from grit particles or rain.

Two items of photographic equipment that are particularly useful on holiday are a lens hood and a skylight filter. The lens hood comes in handy when the light is very bright, at the seaside for example, or on snowy mountain slopes. It will shade your camera lens just enough to prevent stray beams of reflected light spoiling your pictures. A skylight filter reduces the slight bluish tinge which can affect photographs of people taken in diffused lighting or when there is an excessive amount of reflected light about as there is at the seaside or in the mountains. Many photographers keep a skylight filter over the camera lens throughout their holidays to protect the lens from sand, dust and dirt. The filter has no effect on exposure.

Wherever or whenever you go on holiday, even if it is only for a long weekend, it is worth being prepared to take a few flash pictures so that you can take some record shots of hotel scenes and the nightlife.

## Photographing people in towns and cities

Most of the people who holiday in cities like London, Copenhagen, Paris or Amsterdam usually go there to see the sights. A few visitors are more interested in the cultural attractions than in ancient monuments. However, whatever your reason for holidaying in a busy city, you will certainly find that it is the people, the hustle and bustle of commuters and shoppers, the pageantry of ceremonious occasions as well as the antics of other tourists who make the city alive and interesting. It is the people who live and work in the city who create the personality of the place. You may have noticed while on your travels that even in this country, where cities are relatively near to each other, there is a marked difference in character between one city and the next. If you holiday in cities abroad you will find the distinctions even greater.

Photographing the personality of a city is a challenge to any photographer. By far the most stimulating way of doing it is to photograph people doing interesting things. Usually there will be lots of people around and much going on so you should have plenty of opportunities during your holiday to do just that.

You should be able to describe some of the happenings and places you visit quite adequately by taking a single photograph, provided you select your shooting position and camera angles carefully. For example, in London's Trafalgar Square a shot of children, preferably yours, feeding the famous pigeons could quite easily show the National Gallery in the background. However, some of the places you will visit on a city tour will be so busy and colourful that you will need to take several pictures to make a really descriptive account of the event.

While you are being shown round a famous building or monument it can be quite an education to watch the antics of fellow photographers as they frame up and decide whether or not to take the plunge and fire the shutter. How easy it is to spot their mistakes and yet we all do the same things from time to time. There's the man dripping with lenses and a very professional looking camera – the group's moved on and he still can't decide which lens to use; and over there is a young lad shooting away with his lens cap on; whoops, someone's fired a flash bulb, to light a room this size, what a waste ... and so it goes on. As you watch you will surely be tempted to record a few of the weird poses of photographers as they lean and twist and bend to get a better view of things.

Famous shopping areas like London's King's Road are always full of activity whatever the time of day or night for the trendy shops, bistros and discotheques are the Mecca of "with it" youngsters. To capture the free and easy mood of such a place you should try and photograph the shops as well as the shoppers and the off-beat characters. Candid shots are easy to take, particularly if you have a telephoto lens, for no one will hear the click of a camera shutter above the traffic noise. Provided you don't make any fuss you should get on fine. If you want to photograph the shops as well as the shoppers you will need to stand at an angle to the glass so that you can see the display inside the window rather than the scene outside reflected in the glass. This is much easier to do in the early evening when the shop lights are on. However, the artificial lighting will give your colour pictures an overall orange glow which, although not the true colour of the scene, adds to the exciting atmosphere of the place and the people.

Photography in the dim lighting of an evening requires a fully adjustable camera and a steady hand. Exposures at maximum aperture will be in the region of a quarter of a second on a medium speed colour film.

In southern continental cities you may find photography a bit more difficult as you are unlikely to blend quite so well with the crowd. Young people are used to seeing tourists and cameras but women and elderly folk might hold up a hand across their face or simply wave you away. You can usually avoid detection for all but close ups if you have a long focal length lens (not less than 135mm for a 35mm camera).

There is no better place for studying people than from the comfort of a chair in a pavement café. In hot continental cities you can usually get a ring-side seat to view an ever-changing scene of shoppers and tourists, business men and long-haired students. People of all ages, shapes and sizes will parade past your table and provide you with a wonderful opportunity for candid photography. Many cafés are in refreshingly cool, tree-lined boulevards which create ideal conditions for photography. The canopy of trees will soften the light and passers-by will be unhurried and relaxed as they take in the cool air.

A good way of indicating the pace of a city is to photograph people while they are actually walking along so that they reproduce as a blur in the picture against a sharp background. To look effective, you need to create a really blurred impression, a slightly fuzzy outline is usually misconstrued as a photographer's error. If the movement is taking place at right angles to the camera you will need to leave the shutter open for about an eighth of a second to get a completely abstract effect. If you are sitting at a table in a pavement café you should be able to rest the camera on the table to make sure that it is perfectly steady during such a long exposure. If you have a camera with a waist-level viewfinder, you can frame up the scene accurately. If not, you can estimate more-or-less what you will get in. Do put your camera right on the edge of the table, otherwise the bottom half of your picture will be blurred table top.

An alternative way of emphasising the bustle of city people is to use the panning technique described on page 94 to isolate a solitary figure against a background of colourful streaks. To be effective you need to choose a person who stands out from the crowd – you can usually spot someone who obviously enjoys dressing up, every city has its share of dandies, young and old, male and female. Having selected a likely subject, all it needs is a bit of smooth panning to create a colourful picture that has considerable impact. Pictures of people walking across the image area are a good example of shots that call for a horizontal format. A narrow horizontal picture accentuates the impression of movement. To create a picture of this shape with a square format camera you will need to bear in mind when framing up on the scene the final masking of the print.

Pavement cafés and open-air restaurants are ideal places for taking informal holiday pictures of the kids as well as candid shots of the waiters and the occupants of nearby tables. At a busy time of day there is usually so much going on that no one will notice an unobtrusive photographer or hear the click of the shutter above the chattering and clatter. At your own table the children will be far too interested in the exciting new dishes that are set before them and in the general surroundings to bother about the camera. You should be able to capture their expressions and gestures at close range as they discover the delights of the food and turn their noses up at the not quite so familiar tastes.

When the action is about 1.5m from the camera, you will be able to include part of the table setting in the picture foreground; water jugs, wine bottles, menu cards or drinking glasses can be used to frame the picture. You may need to move your props further from or nearer to the camera to create a better effect. You will need to use a fairly low camera angle to "see through" the foreground props across the table to your subject. In the photograph the foreground will probably be out-of-focus and should therefore not be too colourful or obtrusive otherwise it will dominate the picture.

Action pictures of waiters carrying bowls of attractive desserts and cheese boards at shoulder height as they wend their way through the tables need a fast shutter speed to freeze the movement. With a telephoto lens you can capture detailed shots of distant activities and facial close-ups of the staff as they attend to 101 jobs. Such shots will not only remind you of your holiday but also feature in your collection of informal portraits.

In many cities, markets are scenes of great activity. Keen photographers will want to sample the camera potential of the early morning meat, vegetable and flower markets where the shop keepers buy their fresh produce for the day. These markets can be particularly colourful in big continental cities where the trading atmosphere is tinged with fragrance and Gauloise and there is a never ending supply of picture possibilities.

To recreate the air of excitement and to capture the gay atmosphere and raucous colours of the flowers and fruits you will need to use a high speed colour film and to shoot by available light.

You will need to use fast shutter speeds to record in close-up the animated expressions on the faces of the traders when the bidding and bartering is in full swing. In such busy surroundings you will want to make maximum use of foreground frames to simplify pictures and to hide the worst of the background details.

Then, of course, there are the daytime markets which these days seem to have an almost international atmosphere. Whatever city you visit, you are bound to discover another version of the Portobello Road or Petticoat Lane tucked away somewhere in the back streets. Nowhere else in the city will you come across so many colourful and odd characters and so much noise and jostle. You could spend many long hours taking photographs and mooching round the stalls which are usually laden with bargains and bric-a-brac and garish junk. Hopefully, at the end of the day, you will have bagged a good collection of photographs and picked up a few bargains as well to add to the success of the visit.

It's quite fun, while on a touring holiday, to select a particular group of people for pictorial study – continental postmen or policemen usually go down particularly well with the youngsters. If you plan to visit several countries the antics of the traffic police are well worth photographing as their podiums and signalling techniques vary from place-to-place. Picture series like these frequently come in handy at a later date to illustrate the children's school projects when they study the customs of other countries.

Sometimes you can add a lot to a series of photographs with a few shots showing just that people have been there; footprints, litter, ski tracks and so on. Perhaps, too, you can convey the atmosphere of a busy street with a picture of feet, or shopping baskets.

## Pictures at night

As dusk falls on any city the atmosphere changes, on come the bright lights as idling crowds throng the streets waiting for the evening's entertainments to begin. During the summer many cities assume an almost festive air as long hot days draw to a close and people relax in the cool of the evening. Students and youngsters gather in their favourite meeting places, the parks are full of wandering couples and at the gates there is a roaring trade in cool drinks and hot dogs. Suddenly, the crowds begin to thin, as people disappear in the direction of the open-air theatre, the river or the concert hall. Then there is a lull before the final homeward rush begins. Dusk, rather than nightfall, is the best time to take available light shots of people and all the goings on. When it is really dark there is insufficient light to record anything but static subjects. By shooting at dusk on a fast colour film, your pictures will show some detail in nearby figures as well as the colour and impact of the bright lights. A film speed of 160 or 200 ASA permits a dusk exposure in the region of 1/30 second at *f*2.

In low levels of illumination light meters are not one hundred per cent reliable, and readings taken at dusk may result in pictures that are under-exposed or over-exposed. In under-exposed pictures the bright lights will stand out from extra dark and dramatic surroundings. Conversely, in over-exposed pictures the lights will be a bit pale but there will be considerably more detail in the people and the background. If you are really keen to get good results it is advisable to take a couple of shots at different exposures. For example, if the meter reading gives an exposure of 1/60 second at maximum aperture, take one picture at that exposure and another at 1/15 second at maximum aperture. There will be quite a difference in density between the two shots, you will want to choose the one that creates the greatest impact.

When you are taking pictures of people against a colourful background of bright lights, try and compose the scene so that the brightest and most garish colours are not on the outer edges of the picture area. This applies particularly if the background is out-of-focus since point sources of light reproduce as luminous circles, which increase in size as the image becomes progressively out-of-

focus. So what appears in the viewfinder as a distant orange dot will not necessarily be as inconspicuous in the photograph.
And, while on the subject of do's and dont's, remember that lights near to the camera will have more effect on the film in terms of exposure than distant ones. So avoid framing the scene with an attractive old fashioned street lamp in the foreground as it will probably appear as a larger, and far less attractive over-exposed blob in the photograph.
The gay night life in city casinos, clubs and dance halls is there to be enjoyed rather than to be photographed. Strictly speaking you need permission from the management before you can start taking flash pictures and by the time you have sorted that out you will have begun to wish you hadn't bothered. So why not sit back, relax and enjoy yourself, save the film for when you are in smaller, less formal places where everyone takes pictures of the performers and the dancing and joins in the fun.

## Photographing country folk

The centre of country life is the village and in this country every village has a charm and a distinctive character of its own. This is frequently reflected by the local people, in their clothes, their speech and in their friendliness to strangers like yourself.
In foreign parts these distinctions are harder to pin point because everything is so excitingly new and different. It is impossible to detect regional variations in speech and vocabulary when you are struggling with a dictionary and phrase book. However, the language of photography is universal, a camera not only means pictures, it also labels you with a tourist tag. This can be a disadvantage when you are trying to be inconspicuous and aiming to snap up candid pictures of villagers and village life.
In very small villages where everybody knows each other and exactly what is going on, you will find it very difficult to chance upon spontaneous happenings as all eyes will be turned in your direction,particularly if the village is remote and visiting tourists are rare. The only people to totally disregard you and your camera will be the young children and elderly folk. Children are the same the world over – if

they are deeply engrossed in conversation, perhaps telling secrets or planning adventures, they will be far too preoccupied to notice an adult and a camera. You will be able to get in close enough to take detailed pictures of the huddled scene. If their activities involve fast actions you will need to use a shutter speed of at least 1/250 second to freeze the movement in a relatively close view.

It is much easier to photograph elderly folk as their actions are usually slow and sedentary and you will have plenty of time to think about such things as backgrounds and camera angles before pressing the button.

Village festivals and shows, which do so much to maintain the continuity of country life, offer the visitor plenty of photographic opportunities as local choirs, dancers and horticulturalists sport their talents.

Another very English institutions is the village cricket club. Up and down the country weekend matches are hotly contested by enthusiastic players and their supporters. There is nothing more relaxing on a summer's afternoon than to sit and watch and perhaps to take the occasional photograph as the wickets fall and the excitement rises.

In most villages there is usually a place where people congregate to chat and gossip. In this country it is often near the pub or the general store whereas in continental countries the favoured meeting place is frequently the village bar where you will see colourful characters in heated conversation from early morning onwards. It is in places like these that you will have the best chance of meeting people and taking the odd shot of the locals.

If you are touring around the countryside it is always worth having the camera at the ready to record any particularly photogenic scenes that you might come across; a farmer ploughing a roadside field; a shepherd working the sheep with his dog; a peasant leading a team of oxen pulling a laden cart. The possibilities are many if you have time to stop the car and be sociable. But, if you simply lean out of the window and snap timidly from afar, your photographs will surely lack the impact and conviction of a more intimate picture series.

Do take care, though, to keep out of the way when work is going on. Modern farm machinery is powerful and fast. The driver is usually concentrating on several aspects of his job, and quite likely not to be

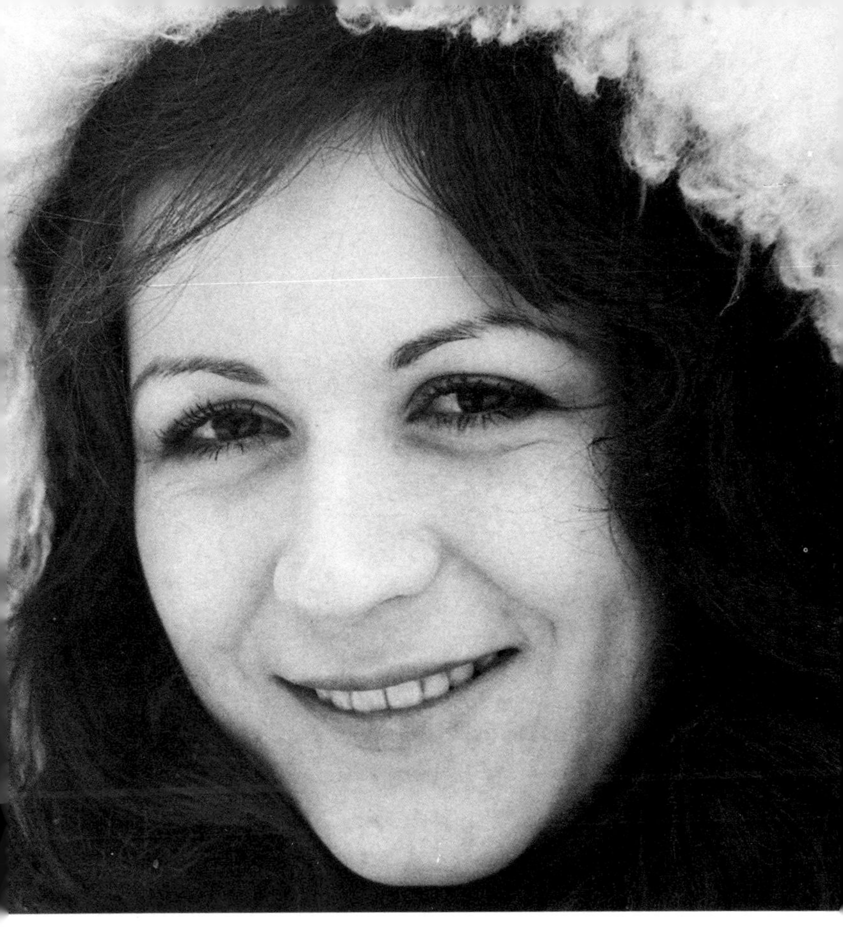

Go in close for full-face pictures. Choose soft lighting – perhaps an overcast sky – and make sure that you focus accurately – *John Rocha.*

*Page 146, 147:* Pretty girls are always good subjects, pay special attention to all other details, though. Posing your model and choosing your lighting is important – *Colin Ramsey.*

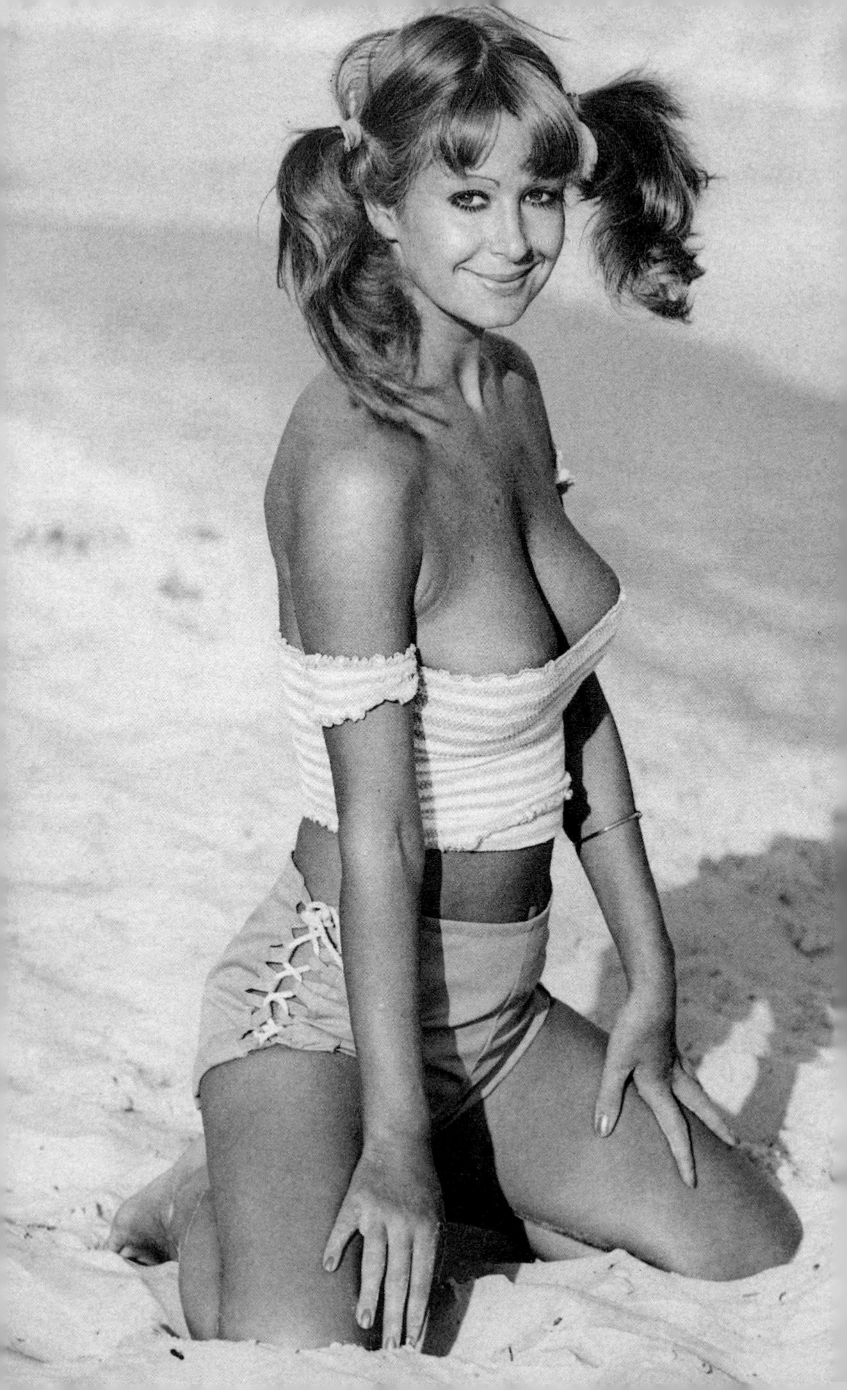

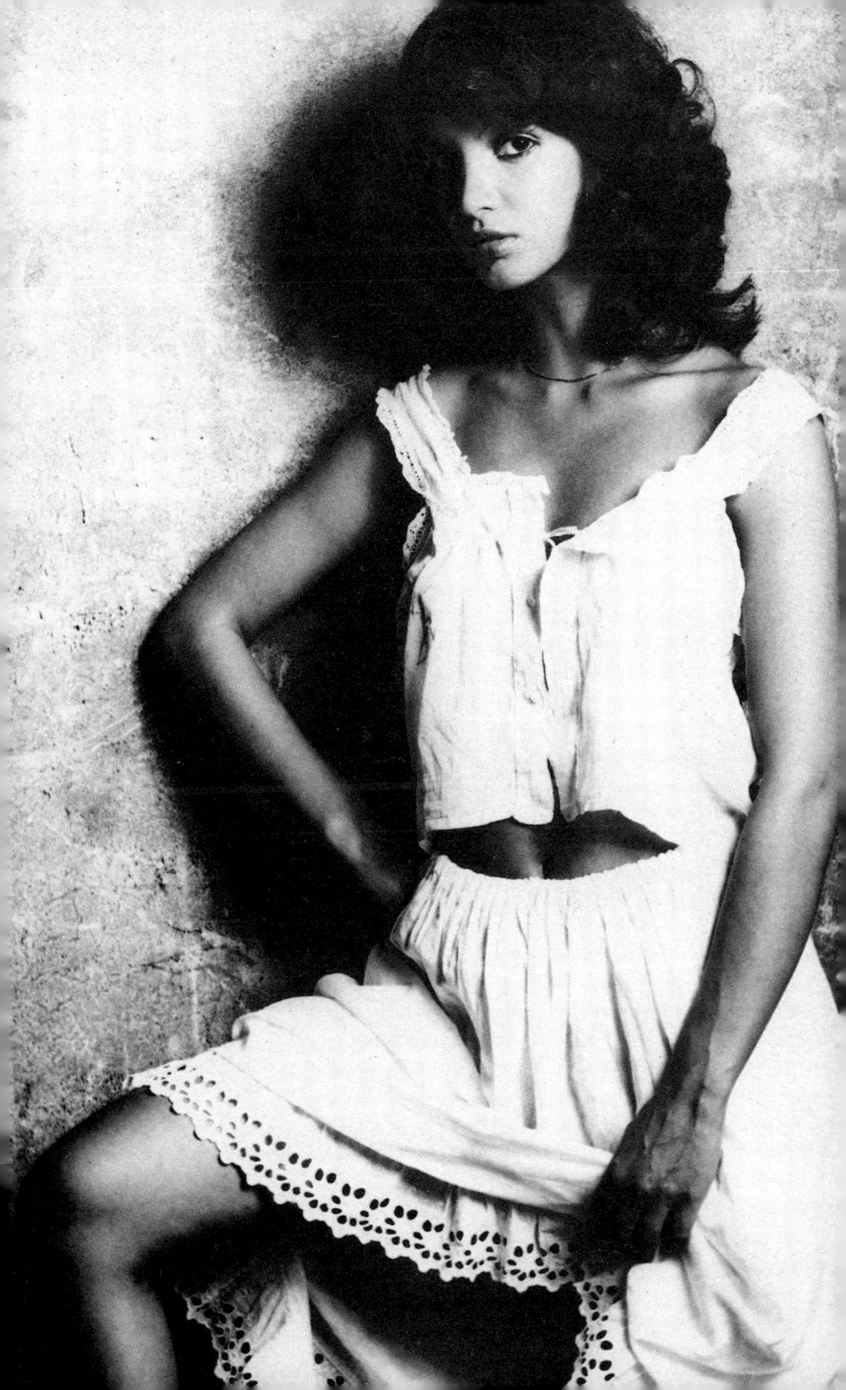

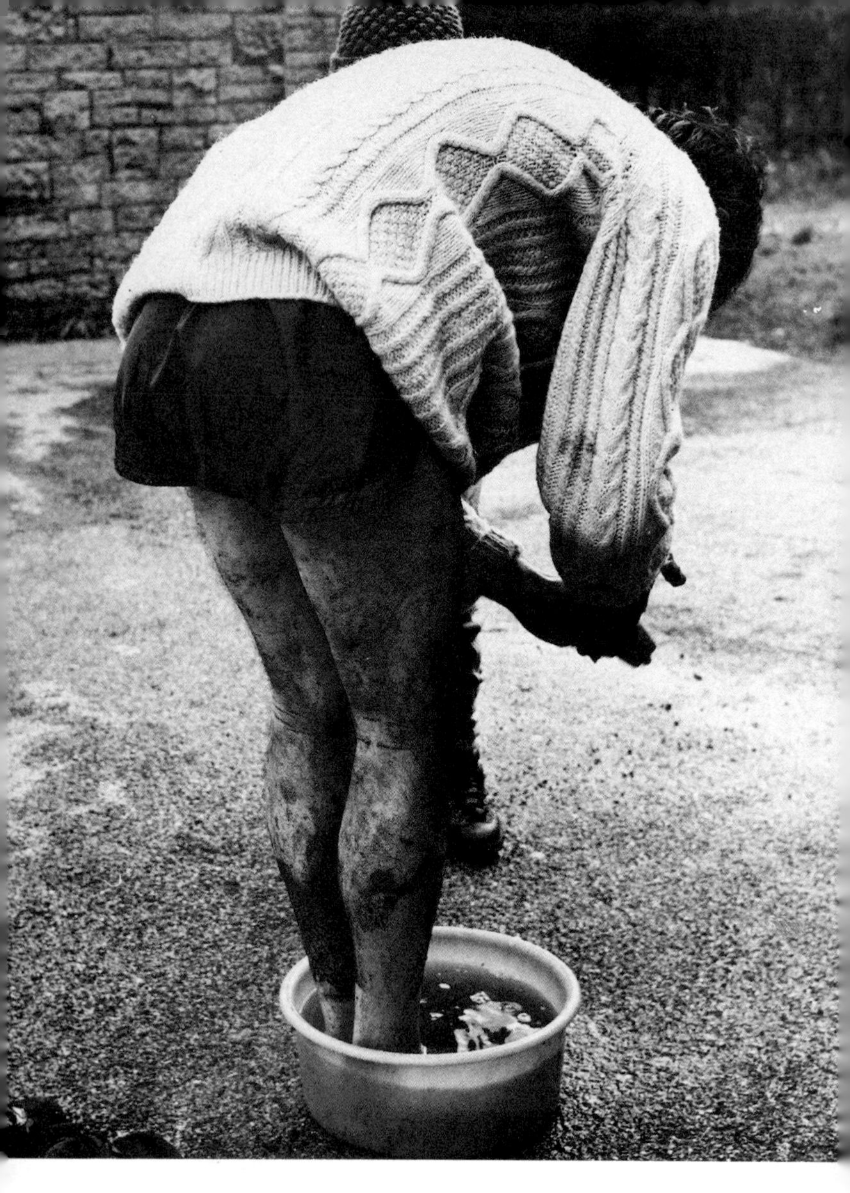

Back views may be as expressive as front views – *Ian Morrison.*

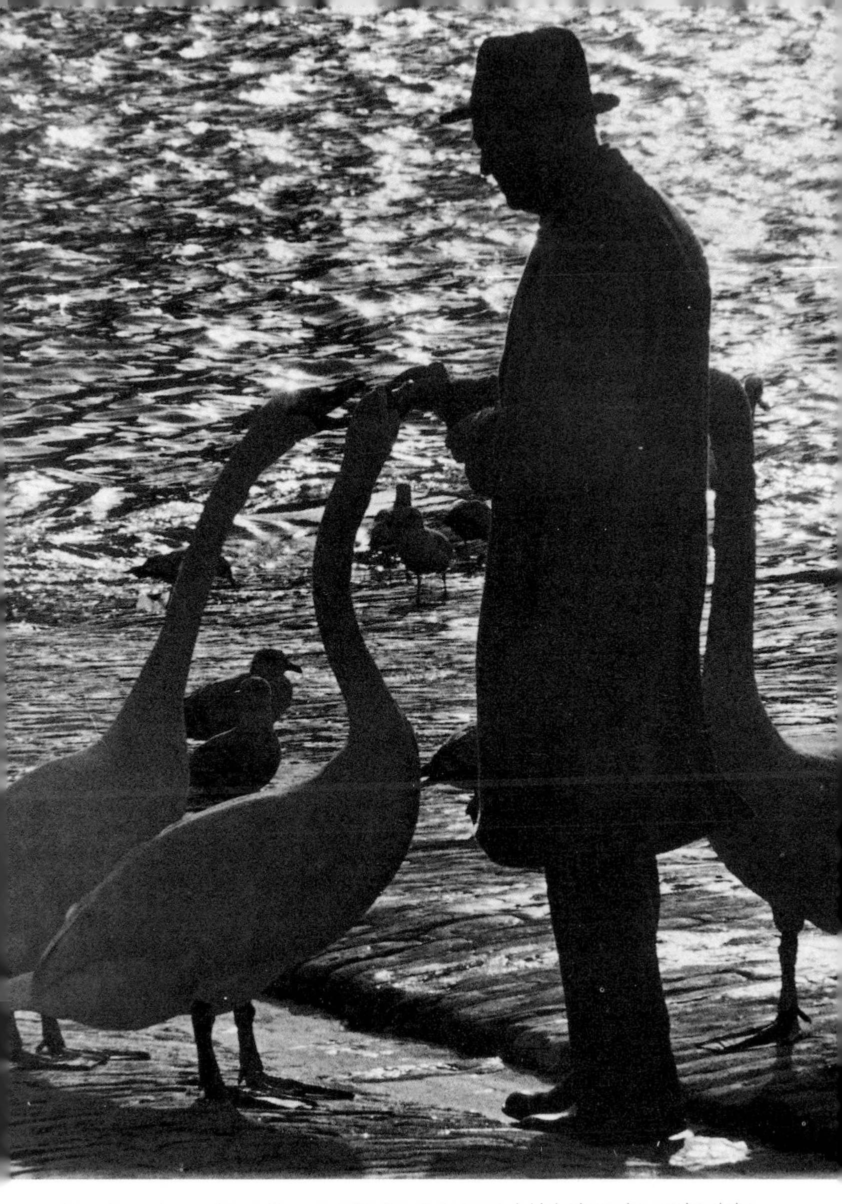

Sometimes, too, a virtual silhouette tells the whole story. A high viewpoint restricted the background to the backlit water – *John Rocha.*

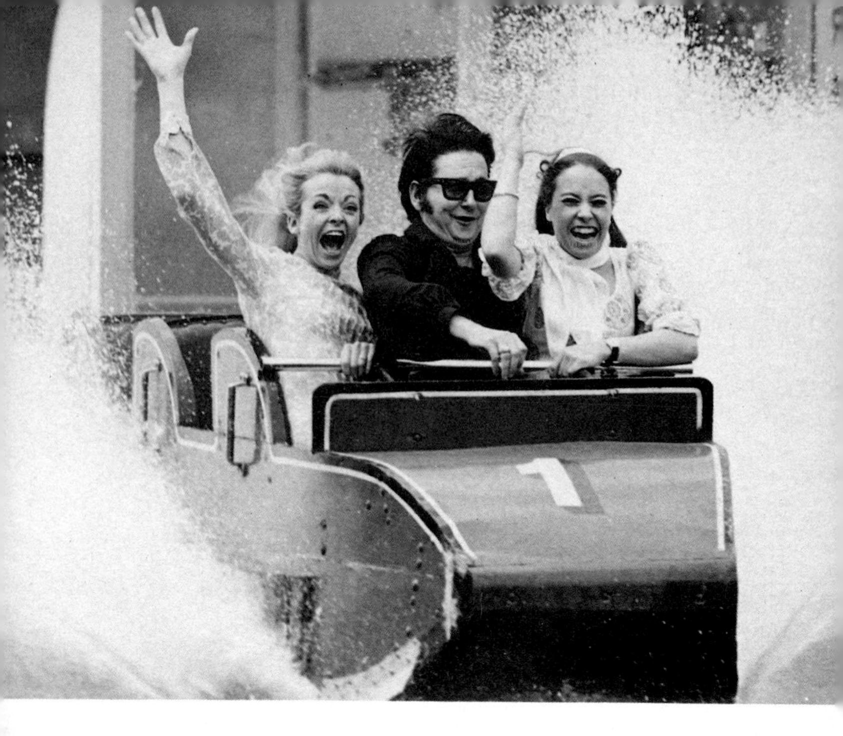

Choose a high shutter speed, and prefocus on a suitable point to prepare your action shots – *Colin Ramsey.*

*Opposite:* People can be a quite small part of your picture, and still be the main point of interest. The surroundings tell a very important part of the story – *Jack Taylor.*

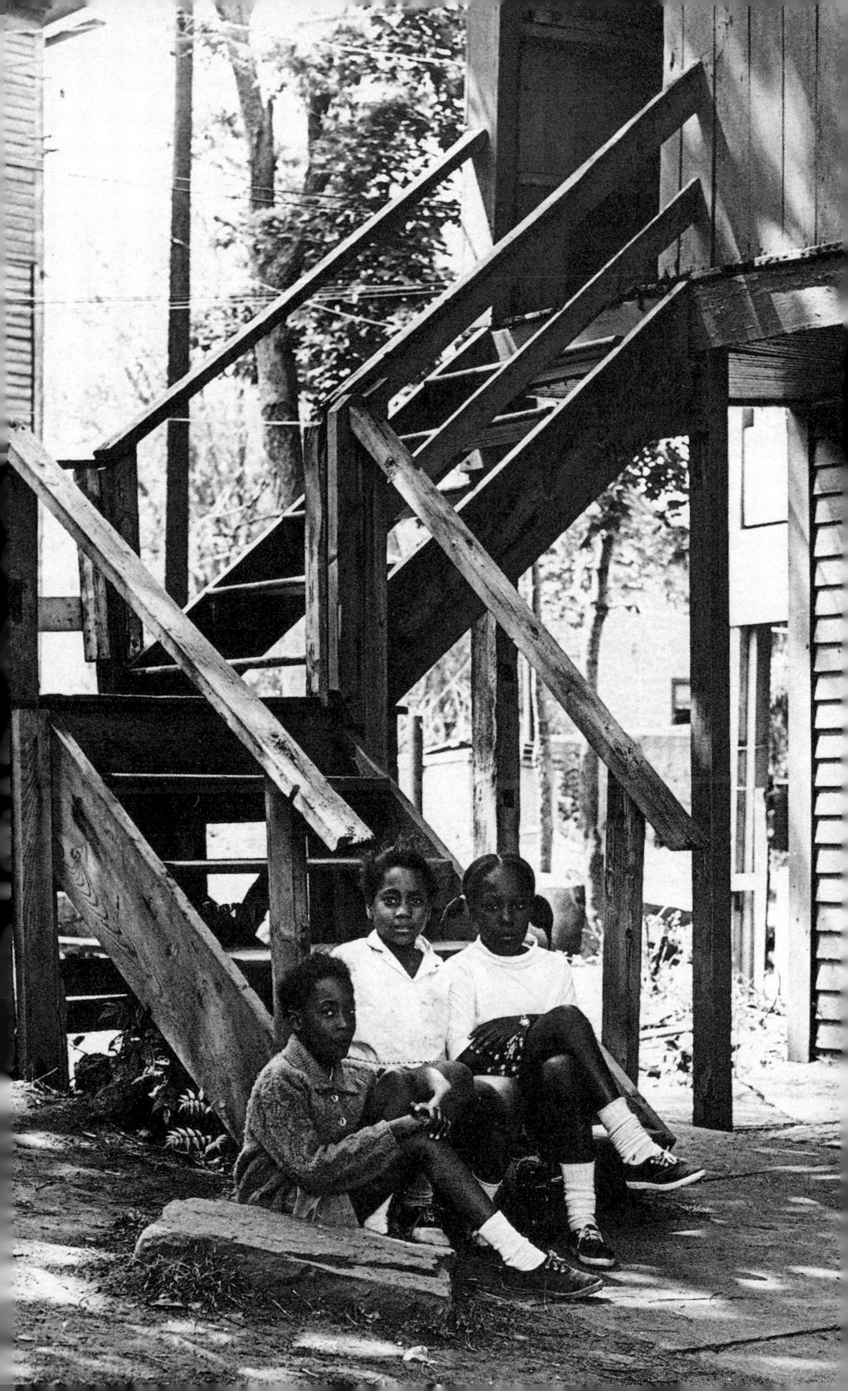

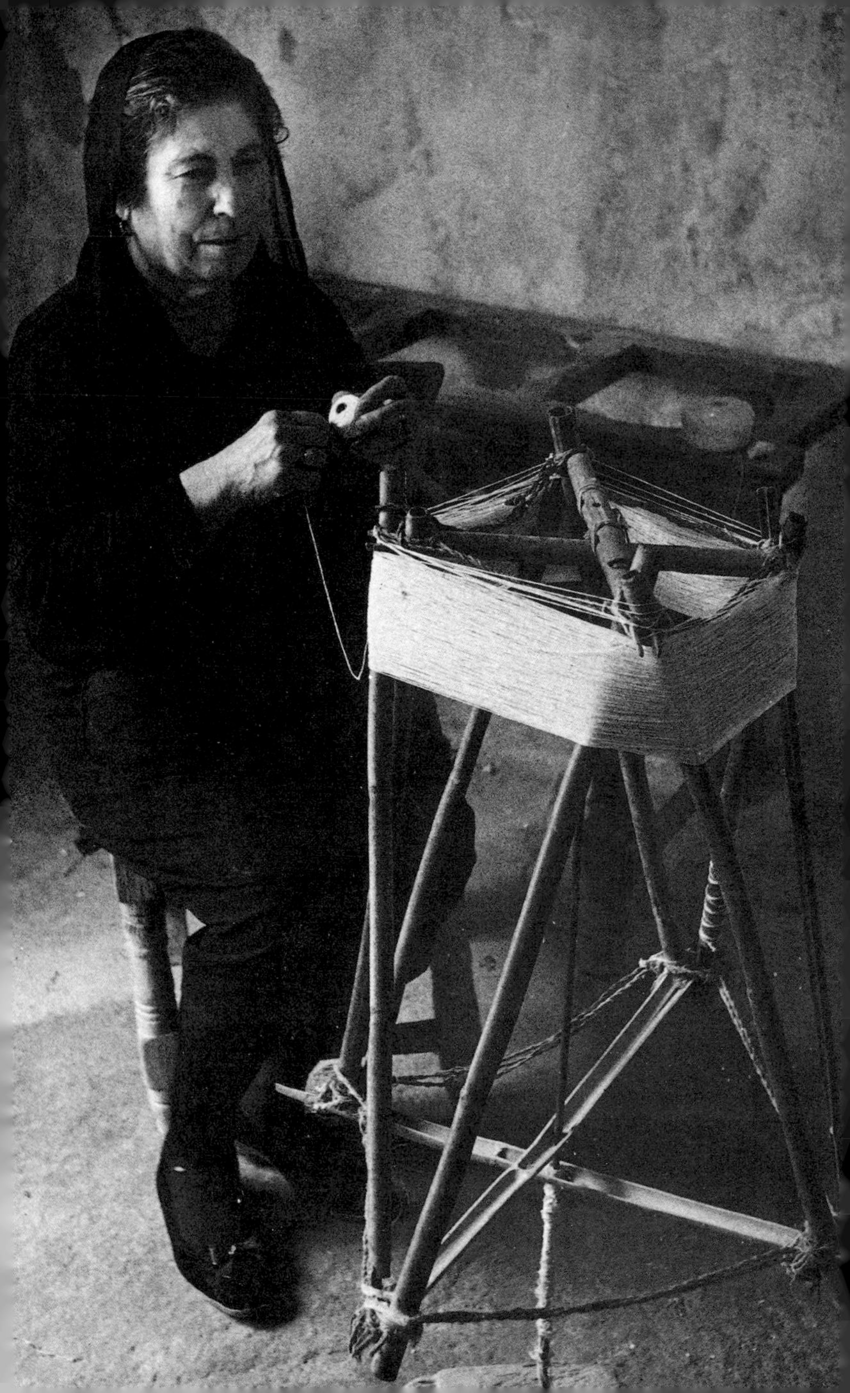

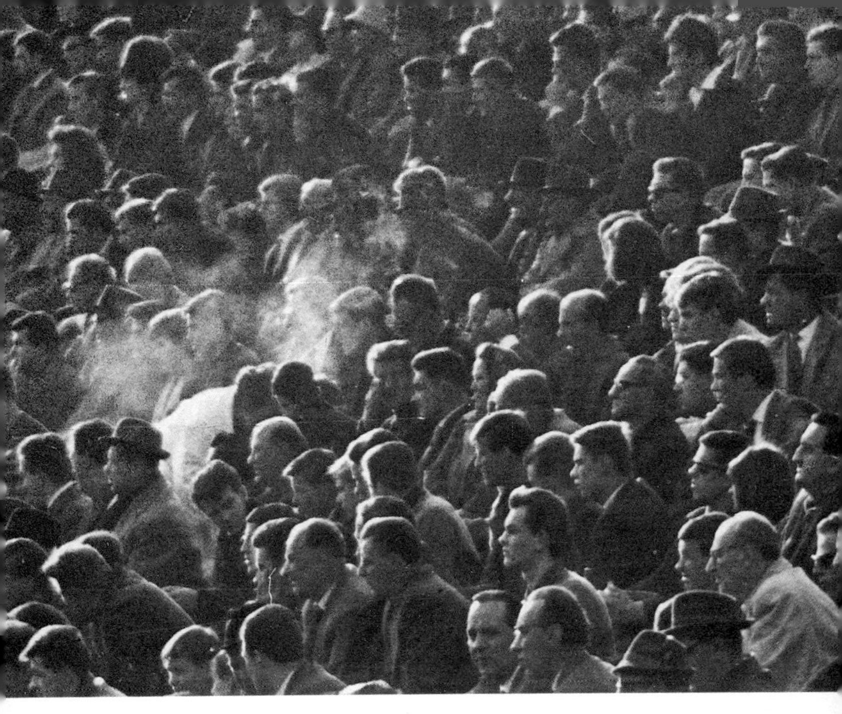

Try watching the spectators as well as the action. This football crowd make an interesting pattern – *Rudolf Kulda.*

*Opposite:* Indoors, choose natural lighting if you can. Focus on the most important part of your subject – in this case the Spanish rug-weaver's hands – *Neville Newman.*

*Page 154:* A detailed background can be an important feature of a picture. The toys are the centre of interest for this little boy – *Jack Taylor.*

*Page 155:* Here, the three girls are so occupied with their toffee apples that any defined background would have distracted from the picture – *Jack Taylor.*

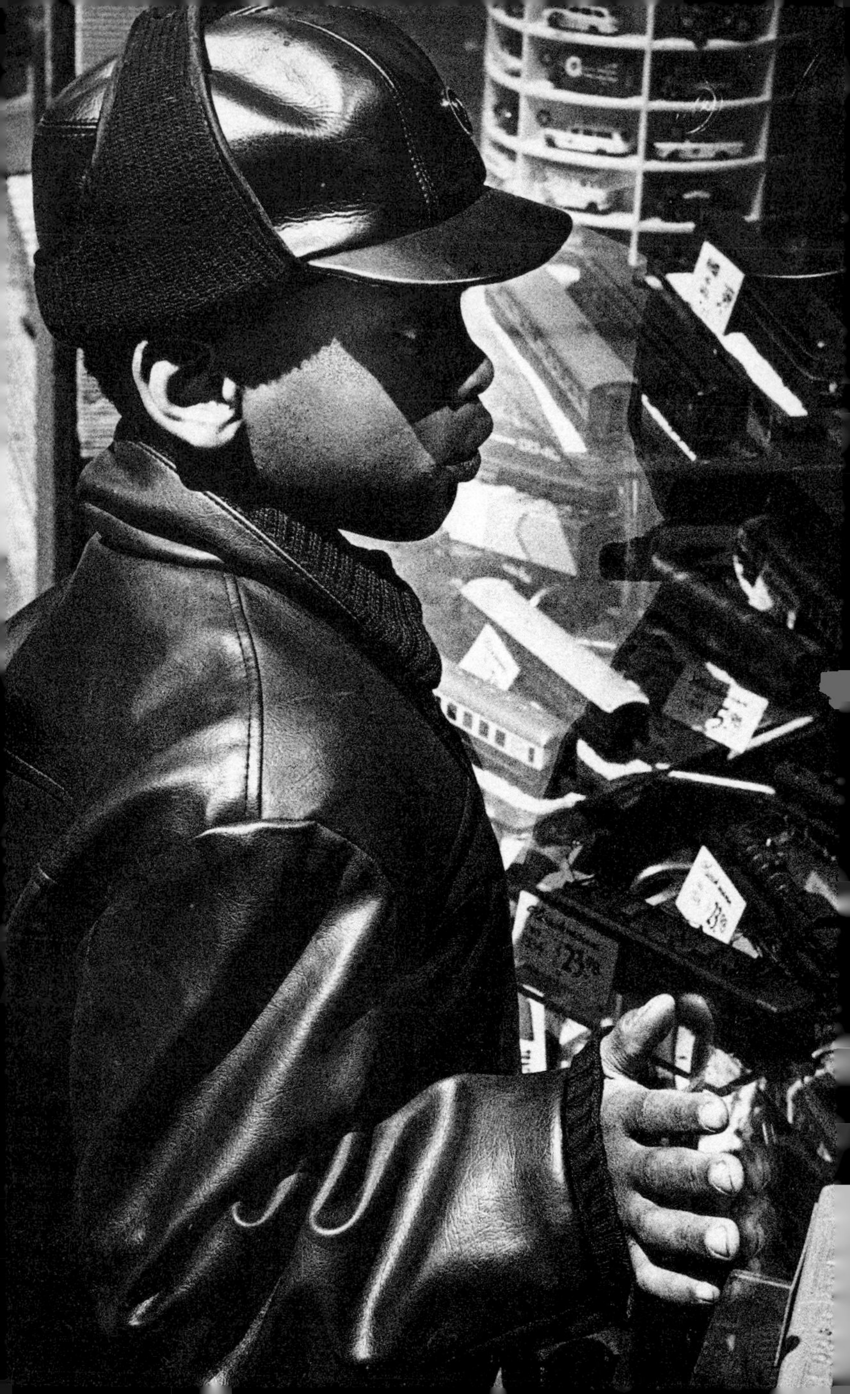

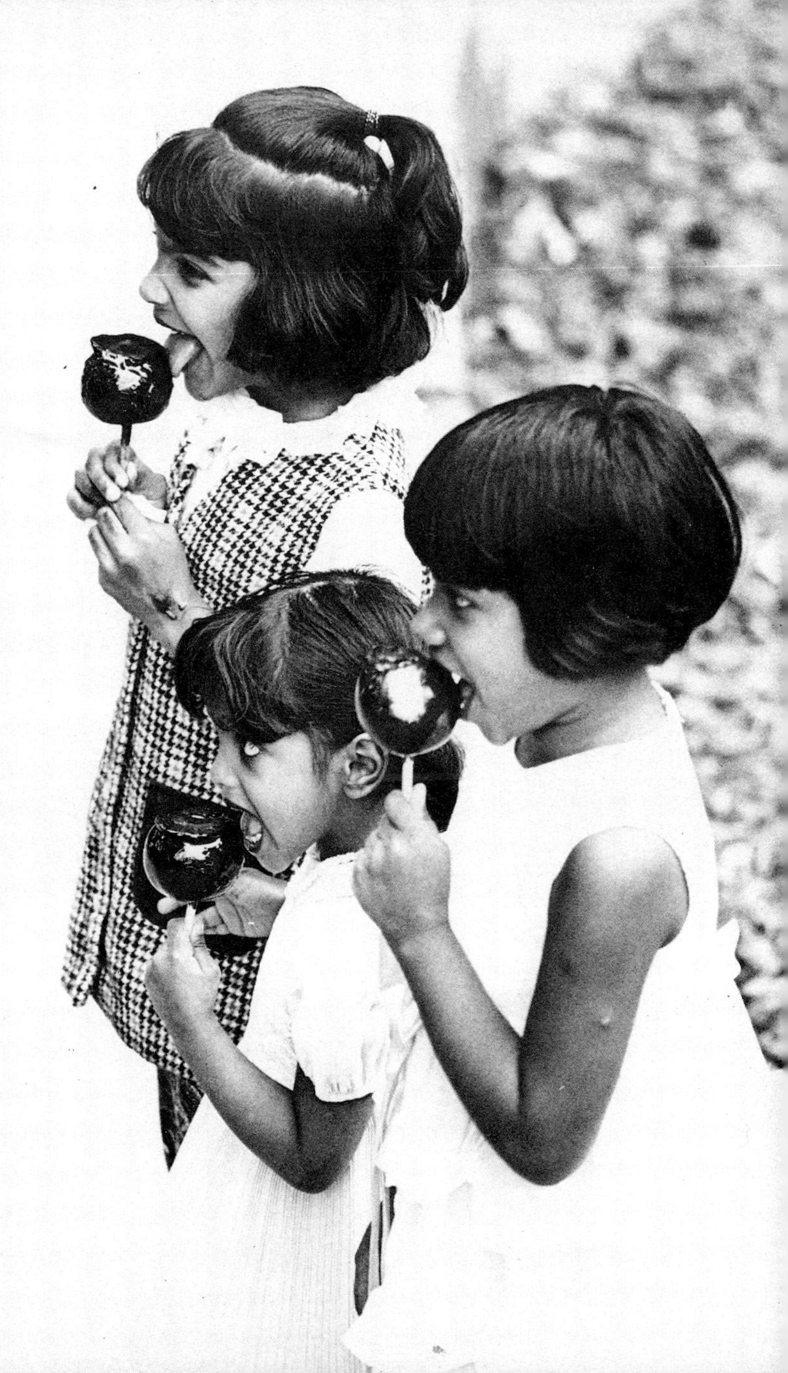

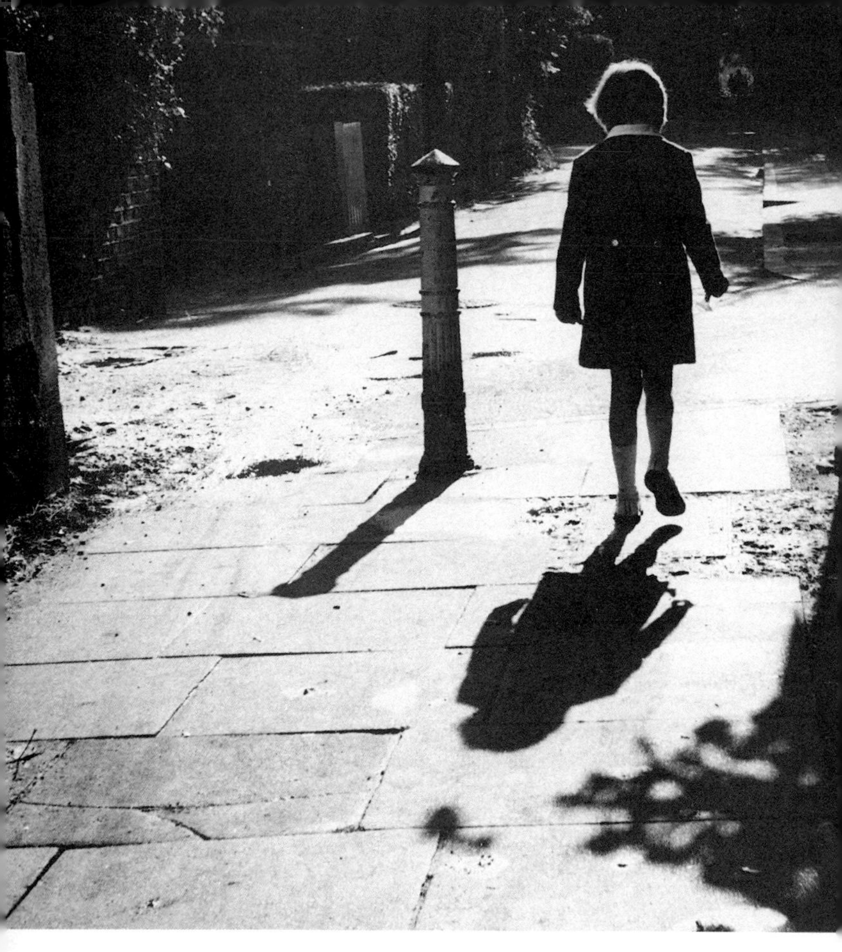

Another expressive back view. Here the strong backlighting has simplified the scene – *Alison Trapmore.*

*Opposite:* Backlighting emphasises movement blur, adding a strong dynamic element to this picture – *Jack Taylor.*

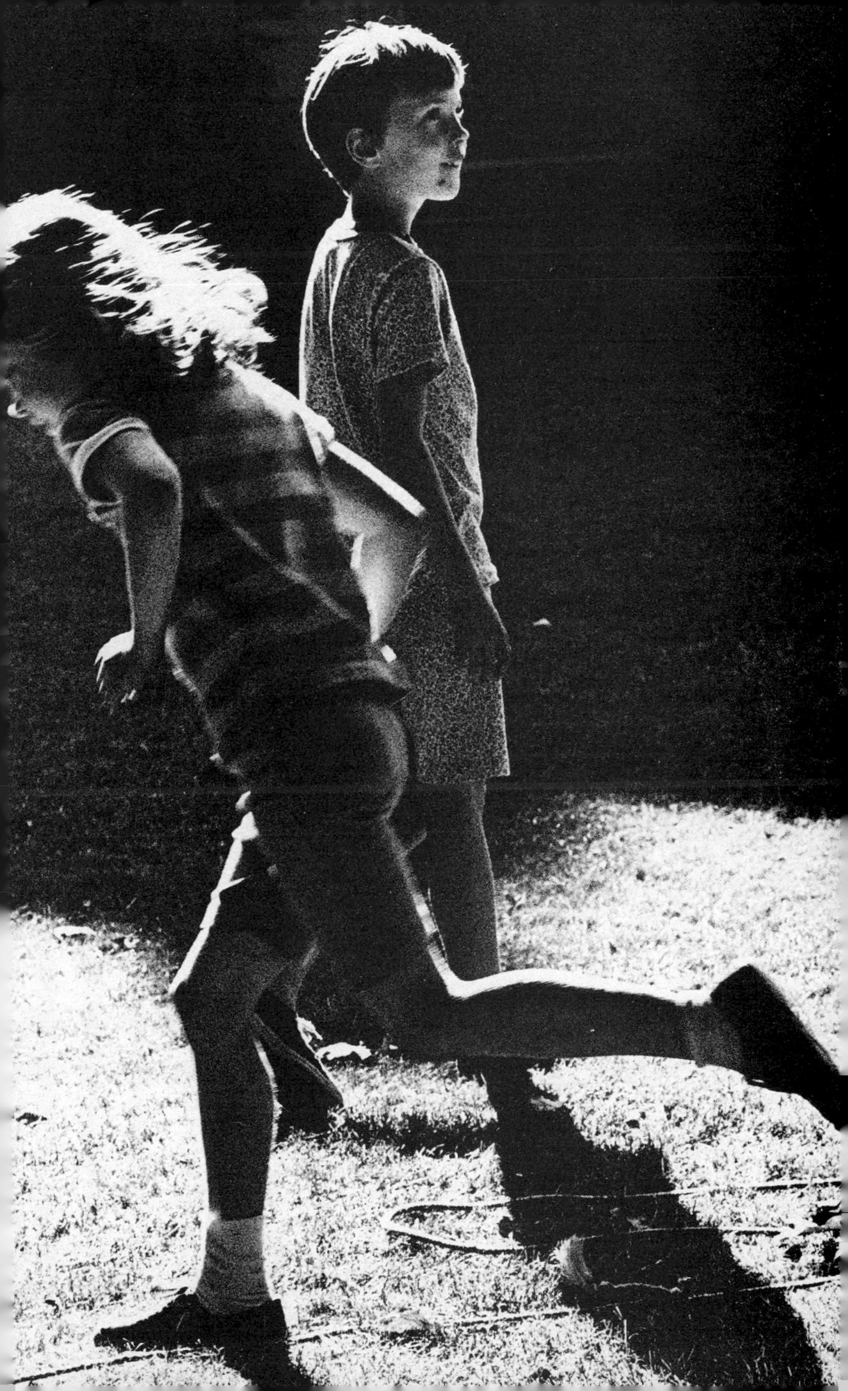

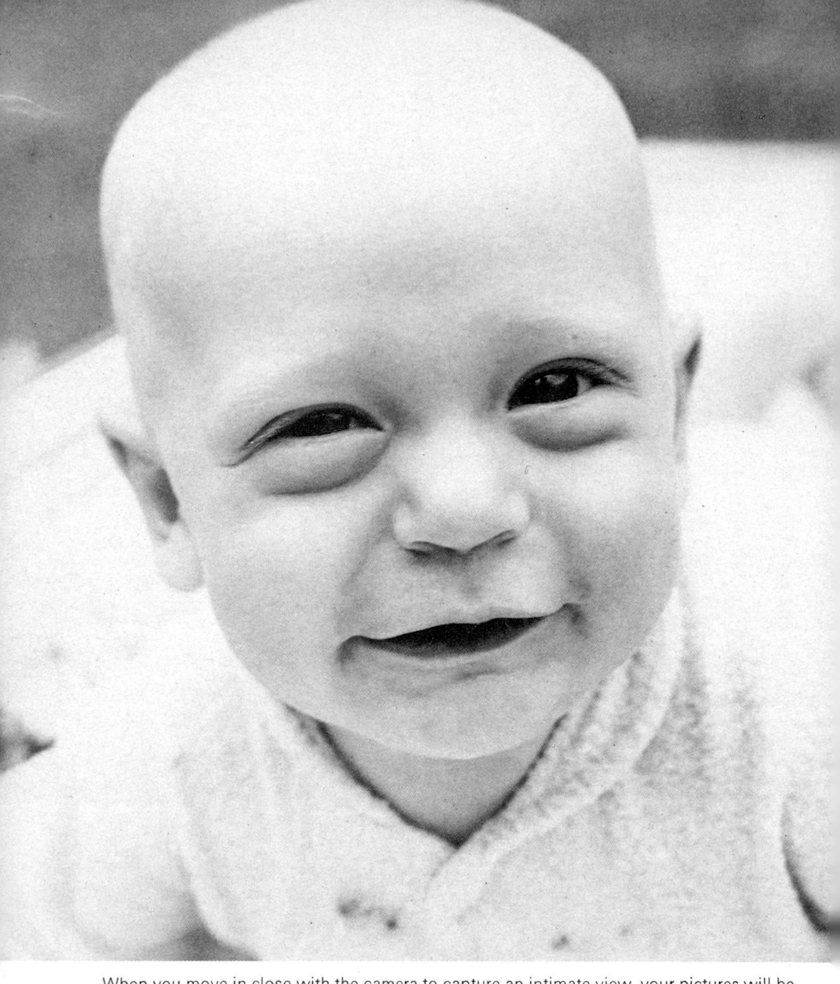

When you move in close with the camera to capture an intimate view, your pictures will be spoilt by the unreality of distortion. Such an effect is immediately apparent if you compare this shot, taken at a camera-to-subject distance of 1m, with the one opposite which is of the same child.

The ideal way of creating close-up pictures of babies is by enlarging part of the negative area.

The simple background in this outdoor shot was provided by a bath towel draped on the grass from the edge of a deck chair – *Alison Trapmore.*

*Page 160:* You can fill your frame with a whole baby without going too close. Once old enough, let him sit up alone – *Alison Trapmore.*

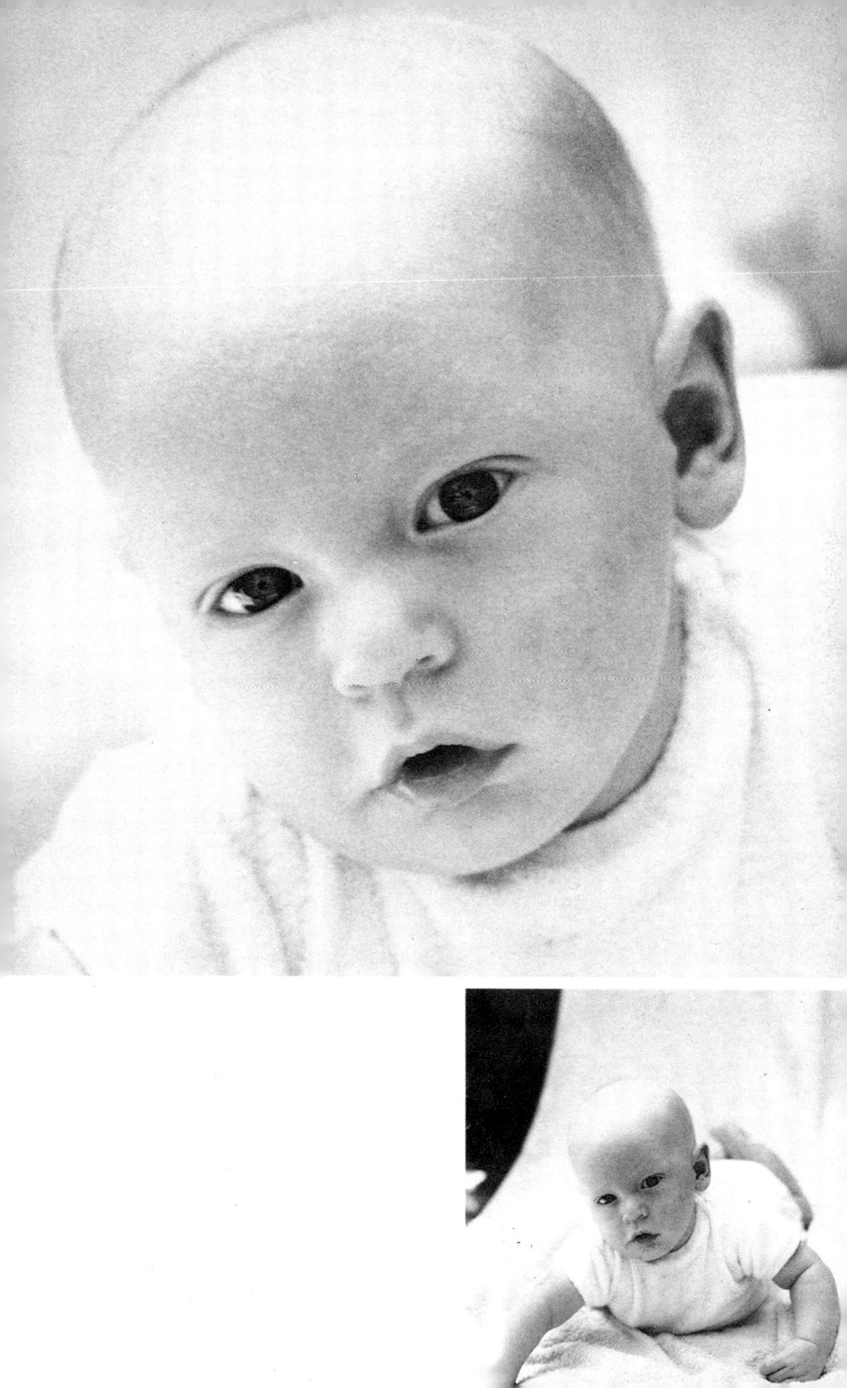

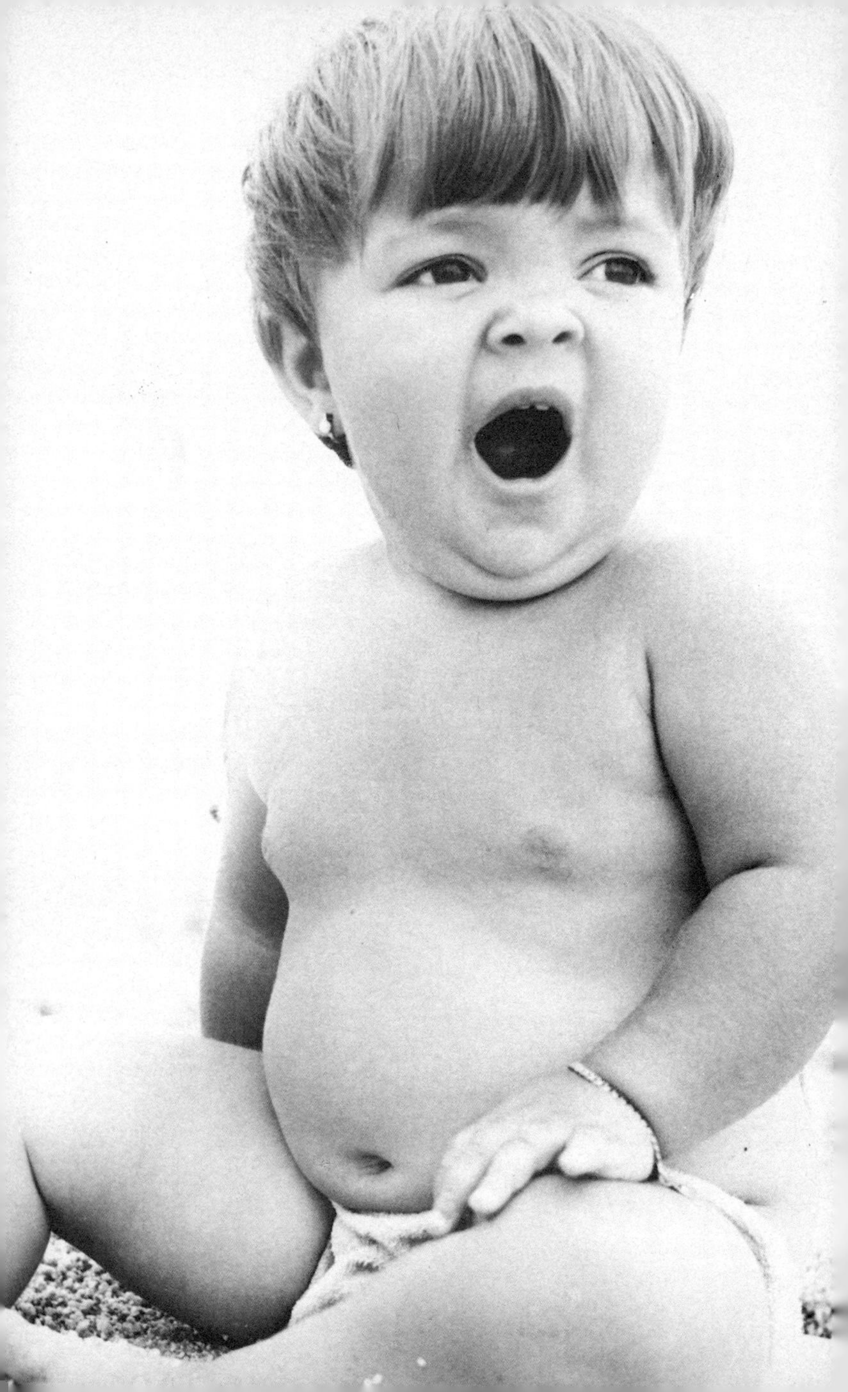

looking where he is going. Even if he does see you, he is not going to be pleased at having to stop or swerve.

## Beside the seaside

Lots of British families spend their holidays beside the seaside which perhaps is not surprising as we are basically an island people. It is our good fortune to be surrounded by 6,000 miles of coastline which contain such a variety of scenery and pleasures to satisfy the inclinations of every kind of holiday maker.
The wide spectrum of holiday amenities provide the photographer with an equally wide choice of camera material. During the hurley-burley of the high season the photographic possibilities are endless. Later on in the year the emptiness and the bleakness of the popular piers and promenades is heightened by the quality of the light as the storms and mists roll in from the sea and the local people recover from the seasonal onslaught.

## On the beach

Children are in their element on the beach for there is no better, or more therapeutic diversion than a bucket and spade and the sand and the sea. Since children are relatively easy to photograph when they are happy and occupied you should have no difficulty in getting in close with your camera and taking lots of good pictures.
If you are buying new play things for your children before you go on holiday, it is worth thinking about the effect these accessories will create in your pictures. Red or orange buckets and spades always look bright and summery, and photograph well against yellow sand. White, green and blue accessories tend to create a distracting element in a photograph as they vie for attention with the child who should be the focal point of the picture.
During the first few days of your holiday you will probably be too busy getting brown to want to investigate all the different things that are going on around you. This is a good opportunity to photograph the children playing on the sand and at the water's edge.

| Event | | Possible Photographs |
|---|---|---|
| Building sandcastles | 1. | Medium shot of the beach before work begins. |
| | 2. | Medium close-up of child decorating the facade with shells. |
| | 4. | Longshot to show the finished castle and the workers having a breather. |
| Learning to swim | 1. | Medium shot of child and parent running towards the sea. |
| | 2. | Close-up of child testing the water. |
| | 3. | Close-up of parent helping to keep the child afloat. |
| | 4. | Medium shot of child wrapped up in towels after the adventure. |

When the children are splashing about at the edge of the sea or playing ball games on the beach you will need to use fast shutter speeds to freeze the movement. Your choice of shutter speed depends on how far you are from the action and on the direction of movement relative to your camera. The fastest speeds, 1/500 – 1/1000 second will freeze movement at right angles to the camera provided that it is happening at a distance of at least 3m (10 feet). If you do not have an adjustable camera with fast shutter speeds you can still get sharp pictures by keeping at a reasonable distance from the action and by shooting from an angle where the movement is coming towards or away from the camera rather than across the field of view.

Crowded beaches are fascinating places if you are interested in people. Nowhere else will you see such a variety of scenes as people unwind and have fun. If you are not too intent on the serious business of acquiring a suntan you will see endless subjects for photography as you walk along the beach. There will be children everywhere playing energetic games and rushing in and out of the sea, fishing for shrimps in rock pools and scaling the cliffs behind the beach; cosy groups of ladies surveying the scene from the comfort of their deckchairs; elderly folk keeping a watchful eye on their adven-

| Glamorous effect | Photographic technique |
|---|---|
| Rounded, soft features | Diffused lighting – on a sunlit beach turn your subject away from the sun so that she is back-lit. By doing so you create a nice rim light which can be very flattering. |
| A slim line | Ask your model to take a deep breath as you are about to shoot. This draws in the tummy muslces and makes the bust firmer, improving both line and posture. |
| A relaxed expression | Carry on talking as you compose the picture. A few tall stories come in handy here plus a bit of flattery to relax the situation. You want your pictures to do justice to a happy friendly girl who's having a bit of fun. |
| A natural pose | You found your model sitting sun-bathing and she was probably relaxed and comfortable doing just that. If you photograph her in that position the situation will look quite natural. Choose a shotting angle that shows off her hair style and facial features to advange. |
| A neat figure | Select a camera position that images the "model's" legs and body equidistant from the camera lens so that her head and feet appear in proportion in the picture. If one is nearer to the camera than the other it will appear distorted in the photograph. |

turous grandchildren and of course the sunbathers who come in all shapes and sizes and provide ideal subjects for the candid camera. When you spot a really gorgeous-looking girl she would probably be quite flattered if you were to mention that you would like to take a few close-up shots of her. Try to work out beforehand how you would like her to sit or to stand and which way she should face, bearing in mind the lighting and suitability of the background. With a little planning you should be able to tackle the situation with tact and confidence and organise some good pictures. The following tips will give you an idea of the techniques used by glamour photographers to enhance the appeal of their models:

Selecting an appropriate camera angle contributes much to the success of a glamour picture. If you bend down and shoot from a low camera angle you should be able to isolate a figure in a sitting or standing position against the sky. However, this is not always possible to do when the beach is really crowded. If there are people sitting fairly near to your subject the best way of creating a simple picture is to throw the background completely out-of-focus so that the detail of distant deckchairs and sunbathers merges into a mottled array of muted colours. You will only achieve this effect by setting your camera to wide aperture and moving in close to the subject. If your model happens to be lying near some rocks you may be able to clamber up and shoot from a fairly high camera angle. From such a vantage point it should be possible to isolate the girl against a background of sand, even when there are other people sunbathing fairly nearby.

On foreign beaches the sand is usually a little whiter and the bathing beauties more scantily clad. It doesn't matter if you cannot speak the language, all you need to do when you come across a super looking girl is to improvise with a smile and point at your camera. At worst she will wave you away but you may be lucky and get the chance of taking some really glamorous shots.

## When the winds blow

Beach scenes, particularly around northern shores, are not always ones of bright sun and bikini-clad figures. But even when thundery clouds roll across the sky you will find some holiday makers braving the elements. On occasions like these, when the beach is a less comfortable, more draughty place, you will find many humorous scenes to photograph as people attempt to promenade against the force of the wind. If you happen to be in the right place when the winds blow you will be able to watch and to photograph sand yachting which is a sport that needs force 9 or 10 winds to really excite the spectators as well as the participants. You will need a long lens and a fast colour film to do justice to this fast sport in adverse lighting conditions. If you have neither, try taking pictures before the competitors set off in their yachts as they are preparing for the race.

If you want to escape from the winds and the realities of life a good place to go is to a fun fair or an amusement park and to join in the laughter and excitement that is generated by the flashing lights, the noisy sideshows and the music of the merry-go-rounds. It is not difficult to capture on film the gaiety and spontaneous fun as holiday makers get carried away by the atmosphere of this illusory world. You will find picture possibilities round every corner, as you stumble over a toddler with his face buried in an enormous pink candyfloss, watch the tough guys screaming round in the dodgem cars or come face-to-face with a live fairy-tale character.

When you are using your camera in a busy place it is best to take as many pictures as time will allow. There is almost bound to be the odd unsuccessful shot as someone steps in front of your camera or jogs your arm as they pass close by just when you are making the exposure. And, when you are taking candid pictures, you have to be prepared to discard the shots that failed because the subject moved unexpectedly and the only thing on the photograph is an empty seat or a blurred image.

Spoilt pictures can sometimes be avoided by the use of a fast film like Ektachrome 200 (200ASA/BS 24DIN) which enables you to shoot quickly even in dull weather. Fast films are particularly useful for capturing the fun at the fair at night. If it is very dark your pictures will show figures silhouetted against a galaxy of coloured fairy lights. Facial close ups are best avoided under these conditions as results are never very satisfactory.

Try some long exposures (up to several seconds) so that the people are silhouetted against a sea of light.

## Fishing and fishermen

Another great place for candid photography is at the quayside when the fishing boats return home with the catch. The fishermen themselves make really good subjects for close-up studies as their bearded, weather-beaten faces are particularly photogenic. The unloading of the fish boxes is an interesting subject for a series of pictures, so too is the sale of the fish from the quayside stalls. Successful photo stories contain pictures taken from different camera to subject distances and from a variety of camera angles.

## Lighting on the beach

The light is extra bright on a sunny beach because both sand and water reflect much more light than average surfaces like grass, roads and brick buildings. Because of the increased brilliance of the light you need to give less exposure than you would normally in bright sunshine. The following table indicates the settings to use with different films:

EXPOSURE TABLE FOR PHOTOGRAPHING PEOPLE ON SUNNY DAYS

| Film Speed | Normal exposure for bright sun | Front-lit group pictures on yellow sand | Back-lit close-ups on yellow sand | Front-lit group pictures on white sand | Back-lit close-ups on white sand |
|---|---|---|---|---|---|
| | Average subject | Light subject | | Extra light subject | |
| ASA/BS 25 | 1/125 *f*/8 | 1/125 *f*11 | 1/125 *f*8 | 1/125 *f*11–16 | 1/125 *f*11 |
| ASA/BS 80 | 1/250 *f*8 | 1/250 *f*11 | 1/250 *f*8 | 1/250 *f*11–18 | 1/250 *f*11 |
| ASA/BS 125 | 1/250 *f*11 | 1/250 *f*16 | 1/250 *f*11 | 1/250 *f*16–22 | 1/250 *f*16 |

If you are using an exposure meter rather than exposure tables for working out your camera settings, you will find a general reading will tend to give pictures of people that are under-exposed by as much as two stops. You will get more reliable skin-tone readings if you take them from the back of your hand or from right up close to the people you intend to photograph. Of the two, the hand method is usually the best one as you can be quite unobtrusive about the whole thing which is usually the best way of ensuring natural, relaxed pictures.

## Looking after your camera on the beach

It is a good idea when you take your camera on the beach to wrap it up in a polythene bag to protect it from sand and sea spray. If you take it in a loaded gadget bag it is safest to wrap each item in a separate polythene bag. Equipment is particularly vulnerable on a windy day when fine particles of sand seem to fly everywhere. If any sea spray gets onto your camera lens and as a result salt marks form, clean them off as soon as possible with a lens brush or a soft, lintless cloth. The easiest way to protect your lens is to keep a skylight filter permanently in position while you are away on holiday. The beach, though, is the one place where you should think twice before taking your camera at all. Decide before you go whether you are going to take pictures; and if you are, choose just the items you need.

Avoid loading film into your camera while you are on the beach because however careful you are there is always the possibility that a particle of sand may lodge inside the camera back and damage one of the moving parts.

When you are taking photographs at the water's edge, avoid getting spray on your camera as the salt will stain or even corrode it. You can remove small amounts of spray satisfactorily by wiping the camera all over with a clean cloth moistened with fresh water, and then drying it with a clean handkerchief. Should you be unlucky enough to drop the camera into the sea, rinse it quickly in fresh water, dry it carefully and take it along to the nearest photographic dealer for expert attention.

## Mountain holidays

Mountain areas such as the Alps, the Pyrenees, Snowdonia, the Rockies or the Cairngorms contain vistas on the grand scale that gladden the heart of pictorial photographers. They are areas of great contrasts where you can find peace and tranquility or excitement and danger – where you can be quite alone or surrounded by activity and excitement.

Throughout the year holiday centres in mountain villages are full of activity and stimulating people. In summer you will meet climbers, stalkers and walkers striding off on their adventures. There will be picnickers setting out with laden baskets for a peaceful day on the cool slopes and the odd bird watcher or botanist bent on spotting and identifying as many species as possible as well as parties of school children following nature trails or mountain walks.

In winter, with the onset of the cold winds and the snow, holiday makers have different pursuits. In the daytime skiing and other winter sports like ski-bobbing – which has become very popular in the last few years – tobogganing, skating and curling are there to be enjoyed, and when the skiing stops, the aprés ski starts and goes on until the early hours.

There is no doubt that the big attraction of mountain areas is the beautiful scenery. To personalise scenic pictures, include family figures in the foreground. The most successful shots are usually those in which the people are wearing brightly coloured clothes. Reds, yellows, and oranges make the most impact and add a touch of warmth, particularly to winter pictures. The pictorial effects of the scenery will be at a maximum when:

1. There are a few clouds in the sky
2. The shadows are long, in the early morning or late evening
3. The scene is side-lit so that the ruggedness of the mountains is emphasised

These days winter sports holidays are very popular with families who have small children. Children, of course, introduce endless photographic possibilities as they are always amusing playing about in the snow. If the centre you are staying in has a ski school for youngsters it is well worth going along just to watch and take pictures. Ski clothes are very colourful and lessons are usually full of fun and action. As you are eyeing a subject with a photograph in mind it is always worth while bending down just to see if you will get a better picture from a low angle with a background of clear blue sky. A low camera angle is frequently used to photograph skiers so that they are effectively isolated against a blue expanse. The viewpoint accentuates the strength and solitude of the skier and, because of its impact, it is the angle frequently chosen to illustrate the sport in the travel brochures.

If you like action pictures, you may find a few 'hot-dogging' enthusiasts performing their amazing tricks.

Away from the ski slopes there is usually plenty of bustle and activity in the villages. In winter it is interesting to see and to photograph how local people cope with normal every-day activities and to record the snow ploughs in action.

For many holiday makers the big attraction of winter sports is the aprés-ski entertainment and fun. Even the serious photographer will want to take a few colourful record shots of new friends and happy evenings as warming drinks revive the spirits after the day's exertions on the ski slopes.

Most of that takes place indoors. So, of course, you need your flashgun. Flash pictures, though, are often short on atmosphere. Whenever the action is slow enough, take on existing-light picture, if you can.

## Lighting in the snow

Snow, like sand and water, is an extremely good reflector of light and, because it creates extra brilliant conditions, particularly in sunny weather, you will need to be careful not to over-expose your pictures. Exposure techniques for photographing people in the snow are the same as those recommended for photographing people on the beach (see page 167).

For really sparkling results you should use a haze filter over the camera lens. The filter absorbs the ultra violet light which is a part of the brilliant reflected illumination in snowy conditions. This light is invisible to the eye but gives colour pictures a blue tinge. These effects are less noticeable in filtered pictures.

EXPOSURE TABLE FOR PHOTOGRAPHING PEOPLE ON SUNNY DAYS:

| Film speed | Normal exposure for bright sun | Front-lit group pictures in the snow | Back-lit close-ups in the snow |
|---|---|---|---|
| | Average subject | Extra-light subject | Extra-light subject |
| ASA/BS 25 | 1/125 *f*8 | 1/125 *f*11–16 | 1/125 *f*11 |
| ASA/BS 80 | 1/250 *f*8 | 1/250 *f*11–16 | 1/250 *f*11 |
| ASA/BS 125 | 1/250 *f*11 | 1/250 *f*16–22 | 1/250 *f*16 |

**Looking after your camera in the mountains**

It is surprising how many people return home from holidaying in the mountains with nothing more than a few bruises and a suntan to remind them of the super time they had because they were reluctant to take a camera for fear of the knocks and damage that their valuable gear might suffer. In fact cameras are pretty robust machines and will come to no harm provided you take a few obvious precautions. These apply particularly when you are on a winter holiday:

1. If you have an every-ready case for your camera now is the time to use it to provide protection from the occasional knocks as you enter the ski lift or clamber up mountain paths.

2. When it is cold and you return indoors with your camera, the change in temperature will cause condensation to form. This moisture will evaporate more rapidly and cause less harm if the camera is left in the open to dry out rather than in the ever-ready case or gadget bag.

3. Fit a haze filter over the camera lens, particularly if it is an expensive model to protect the lens from snow, spray and condensation.

4. If you are a novice on the ski slopes leave your camera behind at the hotel until you have gained a bit of confidence.

5. Keep your camera on a neck strap round your neck fastened inside your anorack so that it is protected from severe cold.

6. While attempting a rocky climb your camera might be safer inside a deep side pocket or a rucksack.

7. Try and arrange your picture taking so that film changes can be carried out in the safety of your hotel room. It is always preferable to load 35mm cassettes in subdued lighting.

8. On normal outings, take the minimum of camera gear with you so that you are not weighed down or inconvenienced by its presence.

9. Do not keep your camera wrapped up in a polythene bag when you are back in your hotel room. Such a bag will harbour condensation and prevent the camera from drying out naturally, should it be subjected to extremes of temperature.

10. Cameras with focal-plane shutters need rather more cossetting than those with the more conventional blade shutters. The shutter mechanism can get a bit sluggish if the camera is left in the cold for long periods. If this happens the shutter speeds will be inaccurate and your pictures incorrectly exposed.

# Photographic Technicalities

Anticipating actions and expressions is just about the most difficult part of creating successful pictures of people. You not only have to develop the knack of being on the spot a few seconds before the action happens, you also need to be ready with the camera to make the most of fleeting opportunities. Whether or not you are able to create a winning shot depends on how quickly you can compose the picture in the viewfinder and release the shutter to capture the spontaneity of the occasion.

Of course there are technicalities involved, once mastered, should become a matter of habit rather than an effort to remember. We have talked about picture possibilities in many different situations, so now here is a résumé of the technical points.

## Checking your camera

If you have not used your camera for some time, or if you want to make quite sure that it is functioning correctly before an important picture taking occasion like a wedding, it is wise to carry out a few simple but effective tests to satisfy yourself that it is working properly. When you have had to search for your camera amongst the mothballs you will need to remove surface dust before you can go any further. A through wipe over the body with a clean cloth should do the trick. The lens needs more gentle treatment with a lens brush or a soft, clean, lintless cloth. A general spring clean should include attention to the viewfinder which can be a great trap for grease and dirt. When everything is bright and clear check that the shutter and the wind-on mechanism are functioning correctly. The last and most effective check on whether or not a camera is in working order is to shoot off a black-and-white test film. Choose a medium-speed film (about 125 ASA) and shoot a variety of pictures in different lighting conditions. Include on the film close-up portraits and medium distance shots as well as long shots of groups of people and, if possible, make one exposure with a fast shutter speed and another at a slow speed.

You do not need to have the pictures printed in order to tell if the camera is in working order. You can find this out if the film is just developed and the single operation will save both time and money. Perhaps you are hesitating at the thought of assessing negative images, if this is bothering you, all you need to do when you collect the processed film from your local photographic dealer, is to explain the problem and to ask him to look at the negatives for you. If all the frames on the film contain an image that is a sure sign that the camera is working properly and, if the negatives all look similar in density to others from which you have had successful prints, you have the proof that you have mastered the techniques of exposure with your camera; and that it is working correctly.

## Lens care

If you have ever worn glasses you will probably be only too familiar with the feeling of satisfaction that you get when viewing the world through freshly cleaned lenses. Once the coating of grime and dust and finger-marks that made everything look so dull and drab has been removed, the day begins on a much brighter note.

Without attention, your camera lens can get just as dirty as the lenses in your spectacles and, when a coating of grime comes between the subject and the lens, the quality of your pictures will suffer. Both image sharpness and colour saturation are impaired because the image forming rays of light are diffused by the layer of dirt. So a clean lens is a "must" if you want to be certain of obtaining the best possible results from your equipment. This applies whether you use a well-seasoned Instamatic camera or a more elaborate single-lens reflex camera.

To maintain your lens in good condition remember to:

1. Use a lens cap to protect the lens when the camera is not in use. If your camera does not have a lens cap, keep it in an ever-ready case.
2. If you are taking pictures in dusty places on windy days protect

the lens with a filter such as a Skylight filter or a Haze filter.
3. Remove specks of dust by gently touching the surface of the lens with a soft lens brush.
4. Remove grease and water marks by gently wiping the glass with a soft, clean, lintless cloth. Never scrub the surface with a used handkerchief.
Note: If the surface of the lens is scratched, one mark will probably not affect the definition in your pictures. The mark will certainly not reproduce on the photograph as a scratch. However, several scratch marks may well affect image quality so it is worth protecting your lens to prevent damage occuring.

## Viewfinder problems

The most common photographic errors caused by viewfinding problems were listed on page 12. These are:
1. That people seem further away in the photograph than you rember them being in the scene
2. An important part of the subject is cut off both at the top and the side in close-up portraits.
3. Part of the top of the head is missing in close-up portraits.
The cause of the first problem is quite straightforward and the remedy is simple. It mainly occurs with non-focusing cameras and is the result of the viewfinder not being positioned right up close to the eye when you take the picture. To use the viewfinder correctly you always want to hold the camera up to your eye so that you can clearly see all four edges of the viewfinder frame. This is easy to do with a focusing camera as it is the only position in which you can focus the image accurately but, when you are using a simple non-focusing model, you don't have to concentrate quite so much on the accuracy of the image in the viewfinder which is why the problem arises.
The other viewfinding problems happen because on all but single-lens reflex cameras there is a physical separation between the viewfinder lens and the camera lens. Because of this separation the two lenses "see" slightly different views of the subject. These differences, or parallax errors as they are commonly called, are only

noticeable in close-up pictures of people when the camera-to-subject distance is down to 1.5m or less (about 3 feet). The actual effect that this has on your pictures depends on the type of camera you are using as you can see the diagrams on pages 177 and 179.

## Non-reflex cameras

It is impossible to achieve really accurate viewing on these cameras so it is a good plan not to fit the picture too tightly in the viewfinder frame at close camera-to-subject distances. If you are taking photographs of a baby for example, the subject should almost but not quite fill the viewfinder frame. There should be a little margin for error around the subject just as a safety precaution in case you inadvertently over-correct or under-correct for parallax at close shooting distances.

## Twin-lens reflex cameras

In the case of the twin-lens reflex camera, where the viewing lens is directly above the taking lens, the parallax difference between the two lenses only occurs in one direction which is the vertical. This means that at close shooting distances, when a face appears in the centre of the upper viewing lens, the taking lens records a much lower viewpoint which does not include the top of the head. Some twin-lens reflex cameras have clear line markers across the top of the viewfinder to remind you to compensate for parallax when you take close-up pictures. Without these lines you simply have to remember when taking close ups of people to move the camera upwards so that the centre of the picture sits fairly low in the frame. With experience of your particular camera you will be able to judge the amount of compensation required easily and accurately.
Another slight viewfinding problem with twin-lens reflex cameras that you will quickly overcome is that of getting accustomed to the fact that the picture you see in the viewfinder is reversed left-to-right. The only time you may find this a nuisance is when you are

taking action pictures which require following movement and fast shooting.

## The low-down on camera settings

*Shutter speeds*: On a modern camera a typical series of shutter speeds is – 1, 1/2, 1/4, 1/8, 1/15, 1/30, 1/60, 1/125, 1/250, 1/500, 1/1000 second. However, because the series contains too many digits to fit on a small dial, manufacturers usually drop the fraction convention and simply write the figures as –

1, 2, 4, 8, 15, 30, 60, 125, 250, 500, 1000

The series may start at 1 second or perhaps 1/30 second depending on the camera. Moving from one shutter speed to the next faster speed reduces the amount of light passing through the lens by half. Conversely, changing to the next slower speed doubles the amount of light passing through the lens by leaving the shutter open for twice as long.

Some cameras also have a "B" setting which is used when exposure times longer than 1 second are required. This oddly-named setting harks back to the old fashioned shutter releases that worked by expelling air from a hand-held bulb. The bulb was connected to the shutter by means of a length of tubing so that the photographer could operate the shutter from a distance. These days a cable release provides the means of remote shutter control and, like the bulb, greatly reduces the risk of camera shake during long exposures.

*Lens apertures*: The intensity of light reaching the film is controlled by an aperture (a hole of known size) in the lens. On all but the simplest lenses the size of the aperture can be adjusted to allow more or less light to pass through the lens onto the film. Lens apertures are calibrated in f-numbers, on a standard scale as follows:

*f*1, *f*1.4, *f*2, *f*2.8, *f*4, *f*5.6, *f*8, *f*11, *f*16, *f*22, *f*,32

Lenses are constructed to give you a range of some of these – within limits, for example, *f*2.8 – *f*16.

To take good pictures of people you don't need to know the mathematics behind these figures, you do however need to remember a couple of details. The first being that the smallest f-

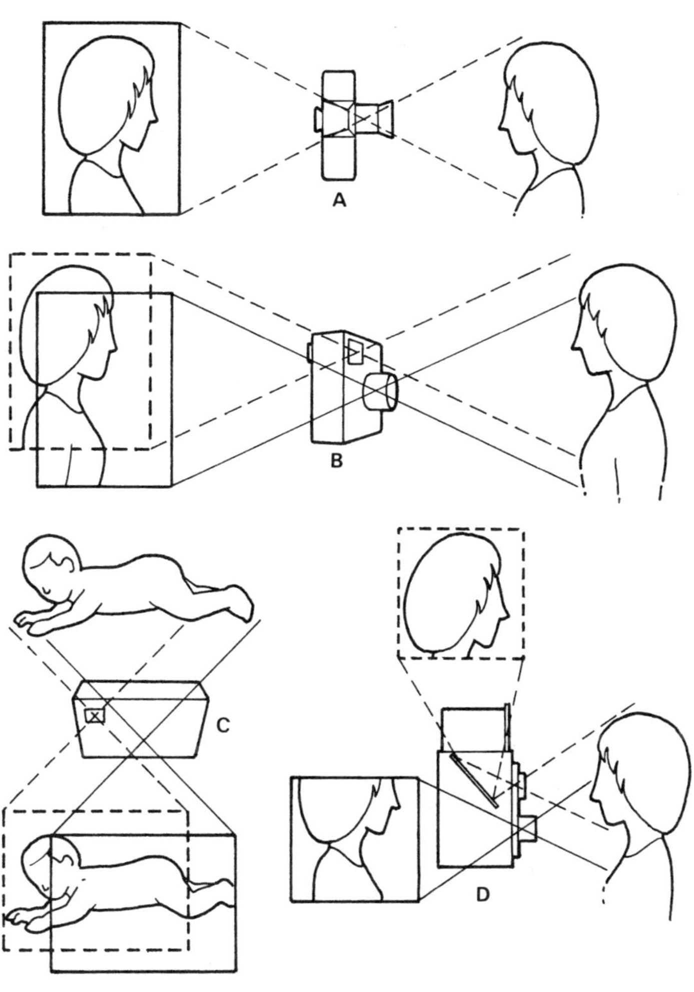


Parallex does not affect the image formed with a single lens reflex camera (A). It is a problem only with pictures taken at close range on cameras that have separate viewfinding systems whether the picture format is vertical (B), horizontal (C) or square (D) as the viewfinder lens and the camera lens "see" the subject differently.

number corresponds to the largest lens aperture and the largest f-number to the smallest lens aperture. The second thing that you need to remember is that moving from one lens aperture to the next larger one (for example, from *f*8 to *f*5.6) means that twice as much light passes through the lens. Conversely, moving in the other direction to a smaller lens aperture (from *f*8 to *f*11) halves the amount of light passing through the lens.

The difference between on f-number and its neighbour is called a "stop". By moving from *f*8 to *f*5.6 you are opening the lens by one stop and consequently giving one stop more exposure. By closing down the lens, from *f*8 to *f*11 you are giving one stop less exposure.

## Setting your camera for pictures of people

Once you have discovered from your film instruction sheet the correct exposure to suit your particular lighting situation you can easily change the shutter speed and lens aperture combination to a more appropriate one to suit your subject.

| Subject | Children at play |
|---|---|
| Desired photographic effect | Sharp image with frozen movement |
| Exposure recommendation on film instruction sheet | 1/125 second @ *f*8 |
| Estimate of shutter speed required to freeze movement | 1/500 second |
| New lens aperture setting to give well exposed picture at 1/500 second | *f*4 |

By changing from the recommended 1/125th second to 1/500th second, you are reducing the amount of light passing through the

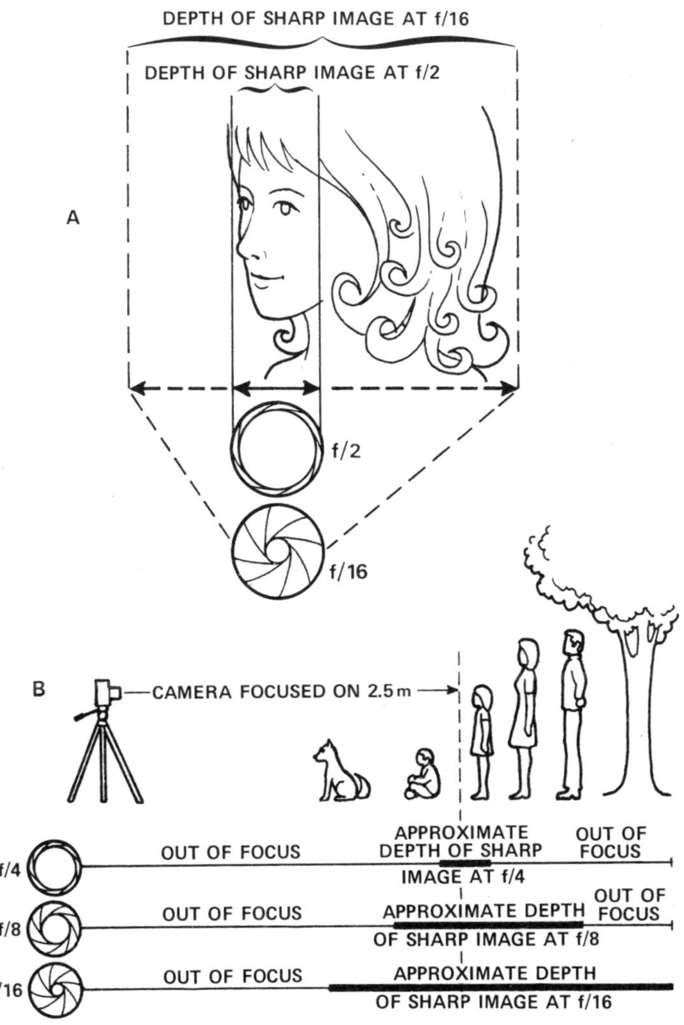


Variations in picture sharpness at different aperture settings, (A) when working close to the subject, (B) with medium-distance shots.

lens by one quarter by moving two speeds up the shutter speed scale. You need to move two numbers down the aperture scale from *f*8 to *f*4 to compensate for the change in shutter speed and maintain a balanced exposure.

In fact, on some cameras the act of changing from one shutter speed to another while at the same time maintaining the correct exposure balance is often extremely simple. The change is easy when there is a mechanical interlock between the shutter and the aperture control rings which maintains the reciprocal relationship between the two at different shutter speeds, once the correct exposure has been set. If your camera does not have this feature, the method of adjustment suggested on page 27 should have the same effect. Of course, if you have a built-in meter, you can set the shutter speed you want, then turn the aperture ring until the meter needle or lights indicate the correct exposure.

## Depth-of-field

Depth-of-field is the term used to describe the distance in depth in the subject which can be imagined in sharp focus by the lens. Many adjustable cameras have a depth-of-field scale on them that indicates how much of the scene on either side of the focused distance will be acceptably sharp at each lens aperture.

If you do not have such a scale on your camera it is helpful to remember that when using a standard lens to take close-up portraits (that is with camera-to-subject distance in the region of 1.5m or 5 feet), the depth-of-field beyond the distance focused on is a little more than in front. The actual distance figures will increase as the camera lens is stopped down. As the camera-to-subject distance increases, so the depth-of-field beyond the focused distance becomes progressively greater than in front. (See diagram.)

The lens on a fixed-focus camera is generally set with a fairly small aperture to give considerable depth of field. This ensures that the entire picture contains a relatively sharp image.

You don't always have a completely free choice in your selection of lens aperture. For example, when you are taking pictures of people outdoors in very dull weather the level of lighting will be so low that you will be obliged to shoot with a slow shutter speed as well as a wide lens aperture in order to give the film the correct exposure. Only when there is quite a bit of light around can you exercise maximum control over the sharpness range of your pictures.

THE FACTORS AFFECTING DEPTH-OF-FIELD

| For maximum depth-of-field | For minimum depth-of-field |
|---|---|
| 1. Use a small lens aperture (e.g. *f*/16) | 1. Use a large lens aperture (e.g. *f*/2.8) |
| 2. Increase the camera-to-subject distance | 2. Move in close to the subject |
| 3. Use a standard lens or one with an even shorter focal length | 3. Use a long focal length lens |
| 4. Make prints with the minimum of enlargement | 4. Make your print from an enlarged section of the negative |
| 5. Use a slow, fine-grain film | 5. Use a high-speed film |

**Zone focusing**

When you are photographing fast-moving subjects such as athletes in action or children at play, or when you are taking pictures in busy situations such as in a crowded market, you often miss potentially good shots by having to stop, focus the camera and set the lens aperture before each exposure.

Photographers who are practised in the art of candid shooting make the most of every opportunity by taking lots of pictures at a fairly rapid rate. They manage to do this by pre-setting the camera focus and lens aperture to give a sharp image over a specific distance or zone in which the subject is likely to be moving. Provided the subject stays within this zone, the photographer can concentrate on composing pictures and pressing the button rather than on focusing the camera.

For effective results you need to bear the following points in mind when setting the camera:

1. The near and far distance limits of the required sharpness zone
2. The lens aperture setting that will provide this depth-of-field and the necessary distance for the camera focus
3. The shutter speed to use at the selected lens aperture setting to give a well balanced exposure with the film in use.

It doesn't always work out that the shutter speed you finish up with will be fast enough to freeze the movement of the subject particularly if the camera-to-subject distance is fairly close and the lighting conditions are poor – allowing you little flexibility in your choice of camera settings. When this happens you have to compromise between the depth of the sharpness zone and the shutter speed. This problem does not usually arise on bright days or if you are taking pictures on an ultra-fast film.

The following example will give you an idea of the sort of distance figures involved using a 50mm lens on a 35mm camera and shooting on 64 ASA film on a bright sunny day:

If the near and far distance limits of the required sharpness zone are 2m and 5m respectively, the lens aperture setting that will provide this depth-of-field is *f*8, The camera should be focused on 3m.

To get a well balanced exposure in bright sun with this aperture setting the shutter should be set to a speed of 1/250 second. This is sufficiently fast to freeze most moving subjects within the sharpness zone of 2–5m.

## Flash facts

These days, what with magicubes, which can be fired without batteries and the easily portable small electronic flash units, flash photography is both reliable and easy. Once you have had a bit of practice with your own portable light source, the majority of your pictures should be successful provided you have mastered the exposure technique and recognised the limitations of flash illumination. The following notes should help you to do both these things, a far more detailed and comprehensive account of the whole topic of flash photography is given in The Focalguide to Flash.

## Flash-on camera

Although flash-on-camera is the easiest and most popular way of taking flash pictures, occasionally photographers are disappointed with some of their results. The following table lists several faults that may spoil the effect of a flash-on-camera picture and suggests simple remedies:

| Fault | Cause | Remedy |
|---|---|---|
| Harsh background shadows | People too near room walls | Have the subject at least 1.5m from the background, shoot from a high camera angle. |
| Under-exposure | People too far away | On a simple camera keep within the recommended flash-to-subject distance range. |
| Over-exposure | People too close | |
| Harsh lighting | Strong flash lighting | Flash-on-camera is not the light for creating good portraits. |
| Burnt-out patches | Flash reflections from shiny surfaces | Don't point the flash and the camera directly at a shiny surface. |
| Red eyes | Flash reflecting from the red inner eye surface | Avoid flash-on-camera for close-up pictures of people. If unavoidable, choose brightly-lit rooms. |

## Bounced flash and Paraflash

With bounced flash, the size of the room and the decorations affect camera exposure and picture quality. The ceilings of very high rooms, found in some houses built in the last century, are unsuitable for bouncing the light as most small flash units simply do not have enough power to travel the distance. The ideal ceiling is about 2.5m

(8–9 feet). It should be white or near white to reflect the maximum amount of light and the room walls should be light coloured. For coloured pictures the reflecting surfaces should be white so that the light they reflect is of a neutral tone. If the reflecting surface is coloured, the people you are photographing will be lit by light of the same colour which, if a cool green or blue, will create an unreal effect in the picture. Warm colours such as reds and oranges produce more acceptable imbalance.
Paraflash, being an independent source of bounced light can be used in any room, whatever the colour of the walls or height of ceiling.

### Flash exposures

*Simple cameras:* To get well-exposed flash pictures the subject needs to be within a particular distance range, anybody nearer to the camera will be overlit by the intense light. Conversely, people beyond the far limit of the distance range will be underlit as the intensity of the flash falls off very rapidly the further the light travels. The distance range varies with different cameras and with the type of film in use. Figures are always given on the flash carton as well as in many film instruction sheets. They are sometimes inscribed on the camera lens barrel.
The flash system on simple cameras is designed so that the flash fires during the time the camera shutter is open and the exposure is being made.
Once you get used to using flash you will find that it does not take long to set your camera correctly and if, for example, you are shooting pictures of people at a party, you will soon find yourself automatically adjusting the lens aperture setting as you frame up on friends at slightly different camera-to-subject distances. In an average-sized room most of your shooting distances will be in the region of 1.75m (about 6 feet). If your camera setting is based on this distance all you need to do is to close down the lens by half a stop for recording pictures of people who are closer to the camera, and open up the lens by half a stop to one stop for more distant shooting. By adjusting the basic setting in this way it becomes unnecessary to perform mathematical calculations before each exposure.

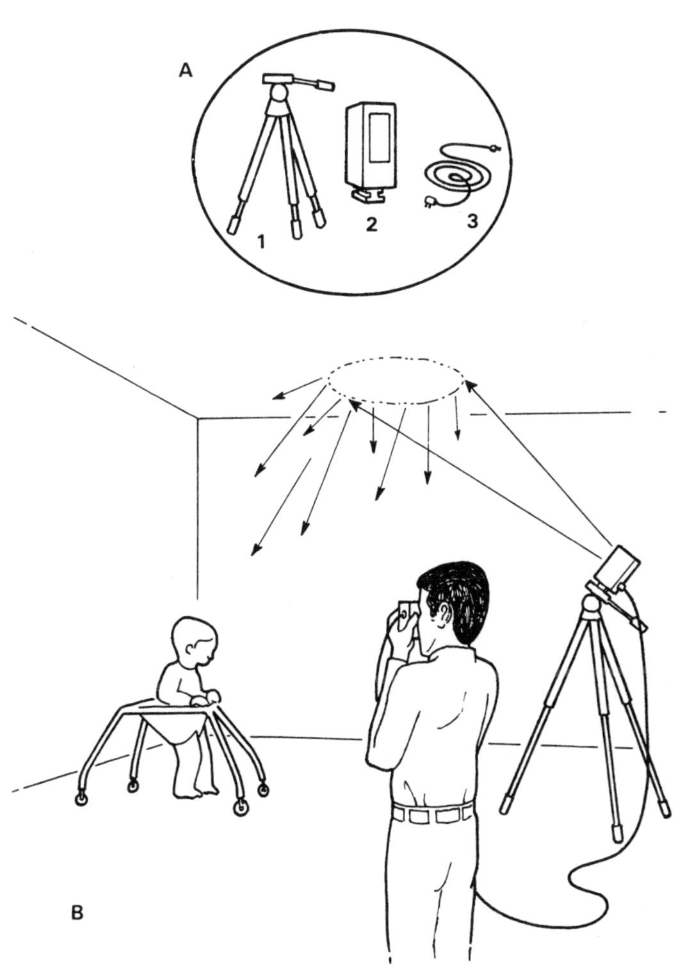


A. Equipment you need for bounced flash (tripod, electronic flash gun, extension cable). B Using the equipment.

*Adjustable cameras*: To get the correct exposure, the shutter speed, lens aperture and flash synchronisation need to be correctly set. The short flash duration normally determines the time for the exposure, consequently the shutter (which only needs to be open for the duration of the flash) is usually set to a fast speed to prevent a secondary image forming due to room lighting and subject movement. This applies particulary when the action happens to take place near to the camera and its effects are more pronounced. Slow shutter speeds are generally used for more specialised forms of photography where the flash is not the whole light source but used to emphasise a particular feature in the scene.

The lens aperture setting is, by convention, determined by dividing a guide number (a figure that takes into account flash intensity and film speed) by the flash-to-subject distance. If the guide number is quoted in terms of metres you will need to estimate the flash-to-subject distance in metres, if the figure is in feet you will be able to tell at a glance if the subject is 5 or 10 feet from the flash. For example, using metric figures, with an electronic flash guide number of 30, a film speed of 50 ASA and a flash-to-subject distance of 2m, the nearest f-number will be 16. With a faster film of 100 ASA the guide number will change to 44 so at 2m the f-number will be 22.

## Flash synchronisation

The different synchronisation settings, "X" and "M", are commonly found on diaphragm shutters: "X" and "FP" on focal plane shutters.

*Diaphragm (within-the-lens) shutters.* With X-synchronisation electrical contact is made just as the camera shutter is fully open. It is the setting to use with electronic flash at any shutter speed and with small flashbulbs, magicubes and flashcubes at shutter speeds up to 1/60 second. These bulbs do not provide such a rapid burst of light as electronic flash and only with the slower shutter speeds can use be made of the whole of the flash.

M-synchronisation is not suitable for use with electronic flash because electrical contact is made to fire the flash before the shutter opens. It is intended for use with flashbulbs, flashcubes and

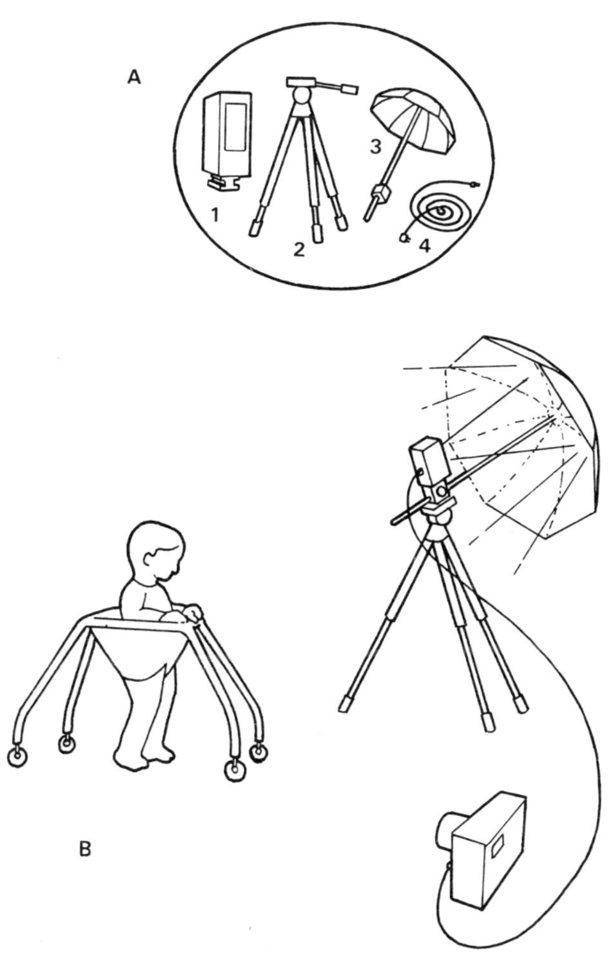


A. Equipment you need for paraflash (electronic flash gun, tripod, photographic umbrella, extension cable). B. Using the equipment.

magicubes at all shutter speeds except with cameras fitted with focal plane shutters.

*Focal plane shutters*. With X-synchronisation, contact is made as the shutter is fully open on slower speeds only. At speeds above about 1/60 or 1/125 second (depending on the shutter construction) the shutter is never fully open. Above this speed (often marked specially on the shutter dial, and always specified in the instructions) you cannot use electronic flash. On this setting you can use ordinary flash bulbs at show speeds (up to 1/30 second). "FP" synchronisation is intended for special slow burning flashbulbs at any shutter speed. It works very like M synchronisation. In fact, most 35mm focal plane shutter cameras produce quite acceptable pictures with ordinary bulbs on FP synchronisation.

## M synchronisation and fast shutter speeds

The duration of useful light from flashbulbs and cubes is in the order of 1/60th second and quoted guide numbers are based on the assumption that you will be utilising most of the light output of the bulb for the exposure.

This is not the case if your shutter speeds are over about 1/100th second. In order to get well exposed pictures with M synchronisation at fast shutter speeds you will need to use a wider lens aperture than the guide number calculation figure suggests. The following table will give you an idea of the amount of correction required.

| Shutter speed | Effect on lens aperture |
|---|---|
| Up to 1/60 second | None – use aperture setting based on normal guide number. |
| 1/100 – 1/125 second | Allow an extra half stop |
| 1/200 – 1/250 second | Allow an extra stop |
| 1/400 – 1/500 second | Allow an extra two stops |

**Exposures with bounced flash**

For each picture divide the flash guide number by the total distance from the flash to the reflecting surface and from that to the subject to get the aperture setting. This is the figure you need to use as the basis of the exposure because you need to allow an extra stop for the absorption of the light by the walls of the room and the ceiling. For example, if the electronic flash guide number is 33 and the total distance from the flash to the subject is 3m, the camera should be set to *f*8 rather than *f*11.

**Exposures with Paraflash**

For each picture divide the Paraflash guide number by the distance from the unit to the subject to find the correct aperture setting to use. Paraflash units are not usually supplied with information on guide numbers however, it is not difficult to calculate the figure for your unit and flash combination.

You need to take a test series of pictures of one of your children or your favourite model on a colour slide film such as Ektachrome-X (64 ASA). Take all the pictures with the unit at exactly the same distance from the subject and carefully position the umbrella so that the shaft points directly at the centre of the subject. Aim the flash straight into the centre of the umbrella. A useful series of pictures would include shots made at *f*4-*f*5.6, *f*5.6 - *f*8, *f*8, *f*8 - *f*11 and *f*11. When you project the processed slides make a note of the aperture used to produce the one with the best exposure. Multiply this figure by the Paraflash-to-subject distance to get the Paraflash guide number.

To find the guide number with a film of different speed multiply the guide number figure you have found with the 64 ASA film by the factor in the following table:

| Film speed (ASA) | 20 | 25 | 32 | 40 | 50 | 64 | 80 | 100 | 125 | 160 |
|---|---|---|---|---|---|---|---|---|---|---|
| Multiplying | 0.56 | 0.63 | 0.70 | 0.80 | 0.90 | 1.0 | 1.12 | 1.26 | 1.40 | 1.60 |

## Available-light photography

Summary of the basic requirements:

1. An ajustable camera with a fast lens and a full range of shutter speeds.
2. A fast film with a speed of at least 400 ASA (fast films should always be loaded into your camera in subdued lighting to prevent fogging).
3. A reliable light meter.
4. A tripod for keeping the camera steady to cope with the really long exposures.

## Exposures in available light

In very low levels of illumination such as in poorly-lit rooms, in candle light or in fire lighting, it is sometimes impossible to record a reading on a light meter. Under these conditions you will have to guess the exposure. However, fortunately in low lighting conditions you are unlikely to face the risk of over-exposing your pictures and so most guesses prove successful.

If you are using a high-speed colour film and the lighting intensity is very low, forcing you to give long exposures, the density and colour of the resulting pictures may not be one hundred per cent satisfactory. That is because the speed of colour films is not constant over the widest range of exposure times. With very long exposures (and with extremely short ones, too) the effective film speed decreases.

Professional photographers use filters to maintain correct colour rendering in pictures taken on some films at shutter speeds over about 1 second. They also allow an extra half to one stop exposure to compensate for the decrease in film speed. Although you are unlikely to require the same degree of colour accuracy as the professional photographer, your colour pictures will certainly benefit if you are generous with exposure guesses when the lighting levels are low. It is often advisable to take two or even three pictures at different exposures when a subject is particularly striking in order to ensure a good result.

## Focusing the camera in available light

If you have a screen-focusing (reflex) camera, focusing is not easy in dim conditions and it takes a bit of practice to create a sharp image when the point on which you are focusing is not well defined in the viewfinder. There are several ways of easing the focusing problem:

1. Fill the frame with the subject so that your final picture requires the minimum of enlargement.
2. Focus the camera on the approximate camera-to-subject distance before using the viewfinder. Then, when you frame up on the subject, move in with the camera itself until the image appears sharp in the viewfinder.
3. Take several pictures so that you are able to select the one in which the image appears sharpest.
4. To ensure that the camera remains steady during the exposure when you are hand-holding it, grip the body loosely with a fairly relaxed arm. The tighter you hold on to the camera the more it is liable to shake.
5. Use a tripod if the lighting is really difficult or the chosen viewpoint awkward for easy camera handling.

## Subjects for available light

If you are short of ideas on what to photograph by available light, have a look at examples in magazines, especially the Sunday press where one of the great exponents of the art, Lord Snowdon, publishes his work. By looking at other people's techniques you will be able to get an idea of the camera techniques used and the wide range of subjects that benefit from the available-light treatment. From looking at pictures you will certainly notice that the images are not always crisp and sharp, indeed, part of the effectiveness of this type of photography is the softness of image outlines which often contrast vividly with the harshness and drama of the situation.

The sort of subjects that are popular for available light photography are:

Elderly people in their homes

Craftsmen at work

Christmas shots of the children by the tree and the fireslde
Musicians performing at dances and concerts

## Window lighting

Window lighting is particularly effective for taking close-up child studies for it is a soft and gentle light providing an extremely flattering effect. In addition, because it is a directional light source, it gives more shape to facial features than such conventional sources of soft lighting as overcast daylight or bounced flash.

The colour quality of window lighting varies according to the outdoor lighting. The only time the lighting can prove unsatisfactory for photography is on a bright sunny day, when the light from the window will contain ultra-violet rays. These will give your colour pictures a blue tinge. However, the effect can be avoided easily by shooting with a skylight filter over the camera lens.

Netted bay windows are ideal places for phtography as the sides of the bay tend to add light to the shadow side (that will be the room side) of the subject. The extra light is usually sufficient to add detail to the shadow areas.

It is possible to use flash to fill in the shadows but, because more pictures have been spoilt by photographers who are unable to satisfactorily balance the daylight with the flash lighting, this method is not advised. The ideal ratio of facial highlight to shadow illumination should be in the region of 8:1.

## Which film?

Your choice of film lies between colour transparency, colour negative or black-and-white and the one you select really depends on what you want.

If you want colour slides for projection and perhaps the occasional colour print of special family pictures you will want to choose a colour "reversal" film. On the other hand, if you prefer colour prints and will only want the occasional transparency then it is much better to use a colour negative film.

## DIFFERENT TYPE OF COLOUR FILM

| Speed category | Availability | Characteristics | Special uses |
|---|---|---|---|
| Slow up to 40 ASA | Mainly 35mm reversal (slide) | Ultra-fine grain emulsions giving brilliant, saturated colours | For photographing people in particularly bright summer lighting |
| Medium 50–100 ASA | Most sizes | Medium-speed emulsions | General pictures of people |
| Fast Over 125 ASA Ultra-fast 320–500 ASA | Mainly roll and/or 35mm | Low contrast emulsions giving soft colour rendition | For action shots and available-light photography |

*Image grain increases and colour reproduction suffers as the speed of the film increases.

If you ever get confused about which are print films and which are slide films remember that the names of most colour slide films end in CHROME and those of colour negative films nearly all end in COLOR. Unfortunately, this is not a universal convention. However, virtually all films have their use marked on the box. Check before you open it and change it if necessary.

Some films can be rated at speeds higher than those at which they are normally used. For successful results the whole film must be exposed at the increased speed. It then needs special processing, which entails increased development, to compensate for the short camera exposure. Your local photographic dealer should be able to give you more detailed information of films that are suitable for the uprating treatment and of local laboratories (or special mailers) offering the necessary processing service.

Of course, you do lose something when you "push" a film. The grain increases, and the colours are often not as good as they are with standard processing.

## Colour slide films

When you look at a colour slide you are actually seeing the piece of film that was previously inside your camera. Since you last saw the roll or casette, the film has been processed, cut up into individual frames and mounted ready for projection. Because there is no further expense of printing and processing involved, as is the case with colour negative films, colour slides are a better buy if you are only concerned with producing coloured images. But, for really first class results, colour reversal films need to be accurately exposed. The main attraction of shooting on colour slide films is the sheer size and impact of the projected picture. There is something extremely eye catching about a clear bold image smiling at you from the projection screen on the other side of a darkened sitting room. And, if the picture is of an appealing subject like a toddler or an attractive young girl, there can be an almost breath-taking potency to the brightly coloured image of a well exposed transparency. Unfortunately you do not get this terrific impact if you view the transparency by holding it up to the light or even when you look at it through a hand viewer, for the picture lacks both size and brilliance when seen in normal room lighting.

Generally, colour transparencies are preferred to colour prints as originals for photomechanical reproduction. They can be used for making colour prints although the results are often not as good as when colour prints are made from colour negatives. In addition printing costs are higher.

## Colour print films

A summary of the advantages and disadvantages of colour negative films and colour prints is given in the following table:

Although colour prints do not have quite the same degree of brilliance as colour transparencies they are certainly capable of creating quite a bit of impact when enlarged beyond the enprint size. However, since colour enlargements are expensive, you will want to select only negatives of your best pictures for such special treatment. You will be wasting money if you send negatives for

COLOUR PRINT FILMS

| Advantages | Disadvantages |
|---|---|
| Negative films give any number of prints or enlargements costing less per copy than those made from colour slides | Colour rendering of mass-produced prints is not 100% reliable |
| Prints can be viewed in normal room lighting | Prints lack the brilliance of colour slides |
| Negative films have considerable exposure latitude and do not require such accurate exposure as colour reversal films | Prints cost more per picture than transparencies |
| Colour negatives can be manipulated during hand printing to give enlargements of outstanding quality | The range of film speeds available in colour negative films is less than in colour reversal materials |
| Colour negatives can be printed on black-and-white paper or on colour print film to give colour slides. | |

enlargement that are smaller in size than 35mm. If you do, you will almost certainly be disappointed in the image quality, particularly if the enlargement is greater than 13x18cm (5x7 inches).

To make certain of really good colour enlargements from negatives that you send away for printing, you need to make sure that they contain the sort of image that will print satisfactorily on a machine printer. Generally, if the colours and the picture sharpness seem to be satisfactory in the enprint, then the enlargement will also be satisfactory. If you are not sure of the enprint or you do not have one, the things to check are:

1. The negative exposure – the best quality prints are made from well exposed negatives.

2. The lighting – pictures taken in bright sunlight that have harsh shadows and burnt-out highlights do not usually make satisfactory enlargements

3. That the image does not contain a large area of one predominant and strong colour because printing machines are designed to make correct colour prints of average subjects that contain an even distribution of colours. They are thrown off-course by negatives that contain an excessive amount of a bright and vivid colour like blue or orange or red and consequently rather unexpected colours result in other areas of the image. There is a perfectly logical explanation for the cause of these odd happenings but since they frequently spoil colour prints it is therefore worth bearing in mind the adverse effects that large areas of colour have on automatic printing machines.
If you make your own colour prints the problem does not arise because you can anticipate the effects of predominant colours and make allowances for them during printing. The same allowances can be made in the individual treatment given to each negative during hand enlarging – a more expensive form of printing service offered by some processing laboratories.

## "L" shaped masks

While you are thinking about the size of enlargement to order, look at the enprint to see if it would be better to enlarge only a selected area of the picture. Experienced photographers use "L" shaped masks to study the compositional effects of different picture shapes. As they are so easy to make it is worth equipping yourself with a pair just to see if they help you to select print shapes that exactly suit the subject in the picture.

To make the masks you need a sheet of stiff card about 30x20cm (12x8 inches). The width of the L needs to be about 6cm ($2\frac{1}{2}$ inches), then if you make the long length 30cm and the shorter one about 15cm you should have a shape that is quite easy to handle. If the card is thick you may need to cut it with a knife and a steel rule rather than a pair of scissors.

To use the masks you simply hold one in each hand by the end of the longer side and position them over the selected enprint or contact print as shown in the diagram. It is very easy to alter their shapes so that you can see the effects of different picture formats.

While you are thinking about the composition of the picture, make sure that the image itself is sharp and that the area you are considering for selective enlargement is not too small. This extra check is needed because the degree of enlargement is going to be that much greater in a selective enlargement than when the entire negative area is blown up to a similar print size. The easiest way of checking negative sharpness is through a magnifying glass.

If you are sending your pictures away for printing you will have to select the nearest standard selective enlargement print area that corresponds to the masking your desire and then trim the

THE DIMENSIONS OF SMALL ENLARGEMENTS

| Film size | Negative or slide size | Enprint size* (cm) | Enlargement size* (cm) |
|---|---|---|---|
| 135 | 18 x 24 mm | 9 x 13 | 13 x 18 |
| | 23 x 24 mm | 9 x 9 | 13 x 13 |
| | 24 x 24 mm | 9 x 9 | 13 x 13 |
| | 24 x 36 mm | 9 x 13 | 13 x 18 |
| 120 or 620 | | | |
| 8 exp | $2\frac{1}{4} \times 3\frac{1}{4}$ in | 9 x 13 | 13 x 18 |
| 12 exp | $2\frac{1}{4} \times 2\frac{1}{4}$ in | 9 x 9 | 13 x 13 |
| 16 exp | $1\frac{3}{4} \times 2\frac{1}{4}$ in | 9 x 13 | 13 x 18 |
| 24 exp | 31 x 46 mm | 9 x 13 | 13 x 18 |
| 126 | 28 x 28 mm | 9 x 9 | 13 x 13 |
| 110 | 13 x 17 mm | 9 x 11.5 | 13 x 18 |

*These are made from the whole negative area less the slight margin required for masking. The ends of a 35mm standard (24x36) negative are trimmed slightly more than the sides.

enlargement to the final area yourself. Selective enlargements from negatives on size 120 film allow you considerable choice of composition. From 35mm and 126 negatives, though, you have much less versatility. You cannot normally have selective enlargements made from 110 size negatives. If you enlarge your own negatives you can make prints to whatever shape you fancy.

The range of small enlargements that are made from various sizes of colour negatives and transparencies generally conforms to standard dimensions. These are given in the table below.

Actual enlargement sizes greater than 13 x 18cm (from oblong negatives) 13 x 13cm (from square negatives) vary with different processing laboratories.

## Black-and-white films

These days most photographers use black-and-white film for one of two reasons – either as an economy measure because black-and-white film and black-and-white prints are not as expensive as their coloured relations or alternatively, in order to learn and practise the skills of the monochromatic art. These not only include the camera side of things but also developing, printing and enlarging. Because the chemistry is quite simple, and the material available, you can try different effects with the minimum of trouble.

It is sensible to use black-and-white film when for example, you are testing your camera or checking your flash gear before an important event like a wedding or when you are experimenting with new techniques that require practise to perfect like panning moving figures or freezing an action when it is at a peak. Black-and-white films are also just the thing to give to a youngster who is keen to learn about photography and consequently rather trigger happy; they are ideal for the teenager who is learning about photography at school or required to take pictures to illustrate special projects.

Black-and-white films that are suitable for photographing people can be categorized according to their film speed as slow, medium, fast or ultra-fast. The performance of films in different categories varies as you can see from the table.

## CHOOSING A BLACK-AND-WHITE FILM

| Speed category | Grain size | Contrast | Image detail | Exposure latitude | Main uses |
|---|---|---|---|---|---|
| Slow up to 40 ASA | Very fine fine | High medium | Well defined | Poor | For studio portraits where print quality is important and enlargements are required |
| Medium 60 to 200 ASA | Fine | Medium | Average | Generous | For candid portraits and general pictures of people both indoors and outdoors in good lighting |
| Fast 250 to 800 ASA | Medium | Medium low | poor | Average Generous | For candid portraits and general pictures of people both indoors and outdoors in winter |
| Ultra fast 1000 ASA and over | Coarse | Low | Poorly defined | Very generous | For picturing people in dim conditions such as by available light; for recording sportsmen in action and for artistic purposes when grain is a feature of the picture |

*Contrast is the range of tones from black through the greys to white that a film is capable of recording. A far greater range of tones can be recorded on a low contrast film than on a high contrast one. An extremely high contrast film will only record two tones, black and white.

**Shopping around for processing and printing**

If you are conscious of the pennies then it is worth shopping around for the best film buys and processing deals you can find, for prices

| Type of camera | Film | Source | Use of pictures | Reason for choice |
|---|---|---|---|---|
| Simple camera | Colour negative | Free film | Family and friends | Service convenient, inexpensive and generally efficient |
| Adjustable camera | Colour slide and b-&-w | Local photo shop | For showing at the camera club and entering photo competitions | The personal contact with the dealer is both encouraging and helpful |

vary quite a bit between the chemist, the photographic dealer and the booming free film organisations whose offers frequently turn up unrequested on the door mat. Which do you choose? If you are a subscriber to the Consumers' Association magazine *Which?*, or can lay your hands on copies in the local library, you will be able to read their reports on different aspects of the subject. As usual they recommend "best buys" and if you don't already have your own favorite film and preferred method of processing and printing you should find the information quite useful.

When there are two cameras in the family, one an inexpensive model which is used for recording pictures of the children around the home which are destined for the photographic album and the other a fully adjustable effort for creative photography, you may find the following approach to film purchase, processing and printing a good one to follow:

Processing and printing your own colour films does not usually save money but it is certainly a very satisfying thing to do.

**Showing your slides**

When you have an evening showing slides to family and friends your efforts will be far more impressive if you have prepared things beforehand. You should try to:

. Show only sharp slides that are well exposed.

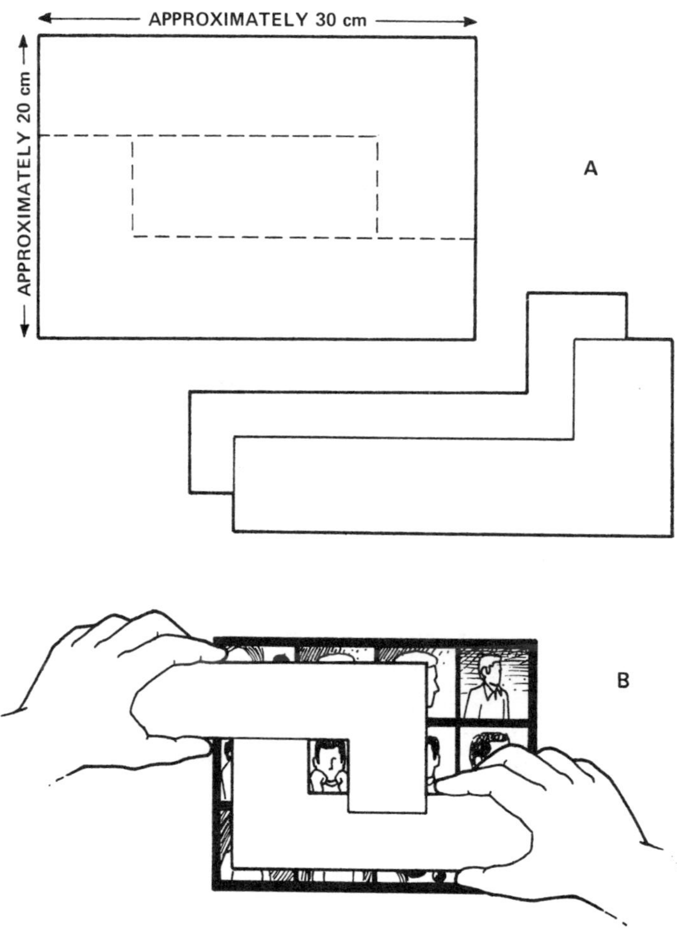


Making 'L-shaped' masks. A. Draw guide lines on a suitable sheet of card before cutting out the shapes. B. Position the masks over the contact sheet or enprint and adjust the shape of the inner rectangle until the most pleasing picture framing is obtained.

. Arrange the slides in a fairly logical order so that there is a series of related shots, perhaps telling the story of a friend's wedding or a day at the fair, interspaced with your best single shots of the children and other pictures of people doing interesting things.
. Have the slides ready and correctly orientated before you start projecting them so that none appear on the screen upside down or back-to-front. The conventional method of marking slides is by thumb spotting (see diagram).
. Run through the slides beforehand just to check that all is in order.
. Keep a spare projection bulb handy – bulbs always seem to choose the most inconvenient times to give up the ghost.
. When you have finished projecting your slides put them away in the same order as you showed them so that they will be ready to show again. If you store them in a proper slide file they will be protected from dust and dirt and individual slides will be easy to locate.

If you have singled out a few really good transparencies to enter into a photo competition it is well worth evaluating your chosen slides along the same lines as the competition judge. He will be looking for impact, good composition and technical quality. Impact and good composition can only be judged subjectively, whether they create a winning shot depends to a certain extent on the actual subject in the photograph. Pictures of people generally create more impact than still-life studies or landscapes, the categories of people with high picture potential were mentioned in Chapter 2. Technical quality on the other hand is purely objective. Such things as sharpness, correct exposure and good lighting are either right or wrong. In prize-winning pictures these things need to be right.

## Making a photographic album

Photographic albums have been around since the advent of popular photography at the end of the last century. Modern albums however, don't have quite the style of the thick, Victorian leather-bound efforts with their ornate clasps and gilt-edged pages. They are more streamlined and practical for displaying a greater number of pictures to advantage. You should be able to see a fair selection of attractive

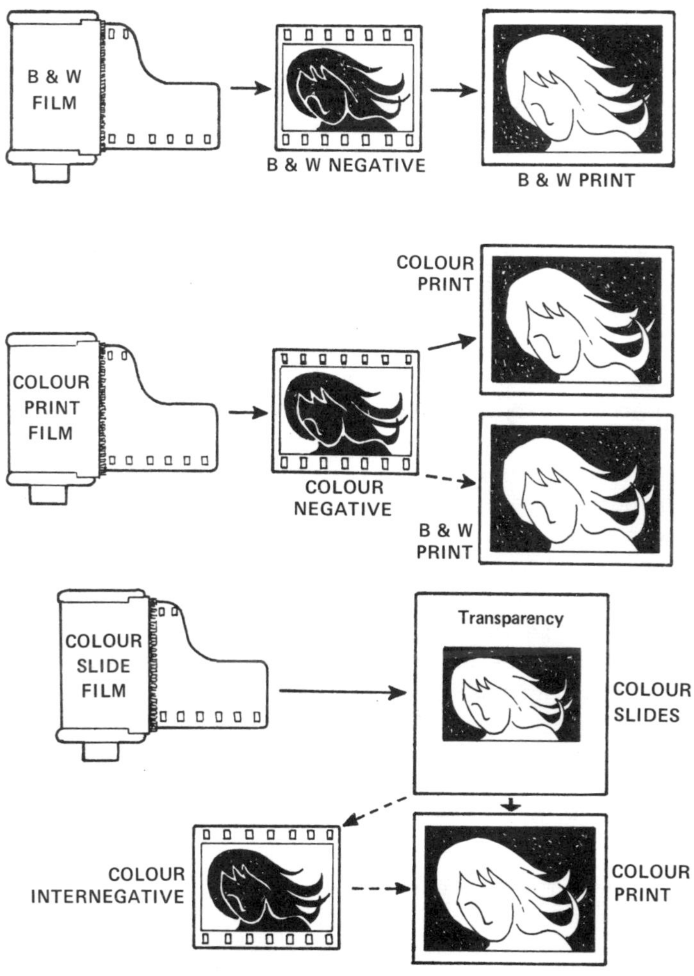


Pathways to pictures with black and white and colour films.

albums on display at your local photographic shop or at any large stationers.

If you go in for doing things yourself, an album is certainly something that you should try making. It is not difficult. All you need is a hard cover (a ring file is ideal) and some sheets of fairly thick paper. An A4 file (297x210mm) is a suitable size as the pages will be large enough to hold several pictures of varying sizes. You can get suitable paper from an art shop. It should be fairly stout so that the pages do not buckle with the weight of the pictures on them. Most art shops have suitable paper in a wide range of colours besides white and black. Colour prints stand out particularly well on a black background. You will probably need to cut the sheets to fit your album – before making the first incision, work out how best to divide up the sheet. (If the staff in the art shop are not very busy when you are making your purchase they may cut the paper for you.) Finally, you will need to punch out the holes to fit the rings. For a neat effect you will want to make sure that the holes are in the same position on each sheet.

One of the most successful ways of mounting the prints onto the pages is by means of double sided adhesive tape (available from most big stationers). To use the tape you simply put a small strip in the four corners of each print, peel off the backing paper and position the print on the page. When you are satisfied with the arrangement, cover the page with a clean sheet of paper (typing paper is ideal for this) and press on the print to secure it to the page.

Caption your pictures as you put them in the album. If you have used black pages you can either use white ink or a special white Chinagraph pencil for inscribing the information beneath the photographs. To add variety to the pages trim some of your enprints and include enlargements of your best pictures. If you are making a baby album you will want to include momentos like the greetings telegrams from your friends, weight cards and birth tags and perhaps to record historic facts like the date of baby's first tooth or his first proper smile alongside the relevant pictures.

You will have lots of fun creating a good photo album and there is nothing quite as satisfying as sorting out a bundle of happy memories. And when Volume 1 is bulging, there will probably be plenty of pictures waiting to go into Volume 2.

## Conclusion

When you are not composing your own pictures of people in the camera viewfinder or sorting out your slides and prints, the best way of finding out about the techniques of good picture taking is to study other people's pictures. Get books out of the library by well known photographers like Henri Cartier-Bresson who is about the most famous candid cameraman, Irving Penn, Man Ray and Edward Steichen to name but a few, look at the picture collections in books such as Helmut and Alison Gernsheim's "Concise History of Photography" and "The Family of Man" which presents a unique collection of photographs of people made by photographers in all parts of the world. In addition, look carefully at the pictures in the photographic annuals and the weekly and monthly photographic magazines.

While you are leafing through a book or a magazine your attention may be caught by a particularly effective shot of a person or a group of people. When this happens try and work out how the picture was taken – what made it effective? Where was the camera? Where did the light come from? You can learn a great deal by analysing other people's pictures and, as you become more critical of other people's efforts, so your own pictures of people will improve because you will find yourself applying the same critical eye to scenes that you are looking at in the camera viewfinder. And there is nothing like a few successful pictures to spur you on to greater things.

# Index